AF413683

REIGN REIMAGINED
(SPECIAL EDITION)

REIGN REIMAGINED (SPECIAL EDITION)

SUMMER N DAWN

Contents

Copyright © 2024 by Summer N Dawn LLC
Cover design by BOOK DESIGNS BY SHAE
All rights reserved. No part of this book may be reproduced in any
manner whatsoever without written permission except in the case
of brief quotations embodied in critical articles and reviews.
First Printing, 2024

To my little support system, who pushes me to reach for the stars.

To my Sunshine, forever and always.

To my Bookish Baddies, who support anyone in the book community and have been there through this process.

To all the inspirational authors, you are the motivation I need!

For all those "handicapable" people out there, always remember you are never alone! No matter what the world says, you are important!

TRIGGER WARNINGS

If any of the following triggers you, please do not read! Your mental and physical health matters!

TRIGGERS:

DEATH

VIOLENCE

SEX

CEREBRAL PALSY

PROFANITY

Always be the Queen you are; no more hiding...

1

Kassani

(June of 2020)

Walking in this gray city that used to be so vibrant, now the street is just lined with me and my thoughts. There was a time when these streets would be elbow to elbow, with no breathing room. Everyone would cough, sneeze, laugh, and spit on you with no care in the world. Recently, people have become reclusive and receive necessities by delivery. They peek out of their windows, watching newspapers flutter down the desolate streets. The joyous laughter no longer exists that used to echo down the alleyways. How could something change so drastically?

COVID-19 hit the world by storm. Everyone fears the many possibilities that could result from the pandemic. The death count continued to rise without a light at the end of the tunnel. People have finally realized that health comes before material items and no item is worth the cost of a life. People continue to live in solitude and have been avoiding contact with outsiders.

As the new world becomes reality, we must change with it. I graduated college with my associate's degree, but I could not handle the new change in the school system. I am a visual learner, but with the new school system, staring at a computer screen just wasn't the same. I would rather be in class, feeling the sensation of human contact and listening to the booming voices. The crackle and pop of my near-death speakers do not allow the same quality of learning that could be accomplished on a school campus. With this in mind, I decided to forgo a four-year degree.

I will be moving into my new accommodations this morning. It may not be the best of conditions, but it has to be better than being among the many scattered throughout the streets. I no longer have the comfort of living in school billeting and must face the hard truth of the real world.

It is time for me to put my best foot forward and make a name for myself in this corrupt, immoral world. Luckily, my family and I have avoided biting the dust through the pandemic, but it does force me to be cautious of everything around me. Masks have become essential in my daily life, along with the trusted 99.9% germ killer that I always keep handy.

My biological parents dare not venture to this tenuousness colossus. Even in this technologically attached world, they have maintained their distance from me. I do not have your typical family. My family was chosen, not given to me by birth. I only claim my chosen family, as they are the ones who have truly cared for me. They are still safely tucked away in their sun-filled little town, which may have contributed to their ability to win the battle against illness. But here I am, braving the streets in lower Chicago. My current living conditions are only temporary and will not stop me from proving myself a worthy and independent woman. I have had moments, as most have, that lead me to doubt myself. All I know is that I am persistent and will continue until this city knows my name. Giving up has not been an option since I was 18 months old.

I was born on a white day in December, healthy and normal, according to society, but God had other plans for me. He figured I could be just a little different. When I was 18 months old, I was diagnosed with cerebral palsy. Later in life, I stumbled on some information that would stir evil thoughts. I could only get cerebral palsy in two ways. The first way is from birth; if someone were born with the cord wrapped around their neck or had any lack of oxygen to the brain, cerebral palsy was possible. But in my case, it was the second option, which was not part of circumstances or natural causes.

The second way cerebral palsy occurs is through violence. A common name for cerebral palsy is shaken baby syndrome. I do not have full control of the right side of my body because someone from my past life attempted to hold me back. Little did they know it only motivates me to be stronger and outpace the rest of the world.

I walk, talk, and perform all actions a bit differently than any normal person. I walk with a limp, and I speak with a stutter at times because I stumble over my words because I can only use half of my brain. Even though many think I am incapable of excelling beyond the average person, I was determined to prove them wrong. I studied harder, stepped with pride, and graduated despite the criticism I had received.

Due to the reality of my condition, I trust no one because the one person I should trust most to love and protect me caused my condition. I do not share my story because certain parties involved would rather pretend that my condition was not due to violence. While they forget and live normally without a care in the world, I struggle to make ends meet.

I have been judged all my life just by my appearance and how I walk, but I am used to it now. This is why I am not scared to start this new chapter here in Chicago. I am ready to get out there, get a job, and send money back to my family. I know people will judge me and think I cannot do anything like they can, but I am here to prove them wrong. My life has been a proving ground for longer than I can remember.

I dated a guy for a year who said he could not handle my handicap tendencies. I laughed in his face and told him that my "handicapped tendencies" could be managed by someone else that was better suited for me. He did not hold back his inner thoughts. He believed that one handicap deserved another, which seemed like an ignorant statement made with the intention of causing mental harm. I ignored that comment since I have been getting comments like that since childhood. People always look at me and say, " Well, at least you are not as bad off as some people." They act like that makes what I go through any better. Gradually, I am learning to deal with these remarks as it makes me a better person. One day, I will find someone who understands me and gives me exactly what I need. Until then, I will focus on marketing myself and spreading my "handi-capable" skills.

I have an interview scheduled for later today. It is 10 AM on a Saturday, and I have finally walked the six blocks to my new apartment. Seven people are standing outside my apartment building, which seemed like a local hangout spot.

I politely scoot past them. A couple of the men commented on my walk: "It's so sad that a cute little thing walks like that."

Of course, I just ignore them. I make my way to the desk in the lobby, give them my ID, and get my keys to apartment number 4A so I can get settled in. The lady asked, "Do you require any special accommodations or assistance?"

I sensed no malice behind the statement, but I could not help my thoughts. I politely smiled, "I do not have many belongings, so I should be able to manage on my own." Making it up four flights of stairs with no elevator will be hard, but I can do it. Thank God for the railings! The lady at the desk lets me know everything I need to know about apartment life. She droned on topics like when rent is due and contacting people if I have any issues. I politely thank her and head up to my apartment. As I head up to my apartment, I notice that the first, second, and third floors are completely full. That makes me wonder if the fourth floor will be as packed.

According to my research, this is one of the nicer apartment buildings on this side of Chicago. The only dreadful thing is they say the landlord is super strict. I could not find much on him. All I found was his name, Massimo Ballentine. My dear friend, Mr. Internet, said he is a very private and rich person. He does not even have a picture next to his name on social media. One of my former friends claimed to have been his date at one of his formal events. She said "it's because he is so rich he must attend different galas." Someone rich likely has an attitude, which reminded me to stay away from him. The lady at the front desk said he barely comes around, except under extreme circumstances. She mentioned she has worked here for 10 years and has only seen him thrice. Hopefully, my stay here will allow me to remain unnoticed by the neighbors and staff, so that I will not encounter any problems.

As I approach my door, I see a tall, burly gentleman leaving my apartment and locking it. With questioning eyes, I look him up and down. You can see the wonder in my eyes—it is like the wheels are turning and not stopping. All the questions are right there in my pupils.

He looks to be about 6'2, with pitch-black hair and has the brownest eyes I have ever seen. I just watched the color change before my eyes. They went from dark brown to caramel brown in an instant. I had to catch my breath before speaking, "Um, hello can I help you? You're coming out of my apartment."

His eyes did it again, they changed color before he spoke. He replied, "Oh! Sorry, I apologize as I was supposed to have everything done earlier before you got here. My name's M! I just had to finish some cleaning and some light maintenance on your bathroom, but everything is ready to go for you. Sorry it was not done earlier."

This man is something else entirely! I bet the lady at the front desk forgot to mention this little detail. "Thank you, M. The front desk lady did not tell me that was happening, she just said everything was in order. Are you sure it was my apartment you were supposed to work on?"

He looks at the floor and smirks, "You are Kassani Carter, right? You are in Apartment 4A, correct?"

Why does it feel as though this man has committed my name to memory? That is crazy to me. I gather my bearings before I answer him, "Yes, that is me; what all did you have to fix, M? I was told on the phone two days ago that everything was ready; were they mistaken? Did something happen?"

He smirked again. What is with all the smirking? He is starting to get under my skin. "Two days ago, Sarah at the front desk called me to double-check and ensure everything was clean and tidy and that no maintenance was needed before you arrived. I have two jobs and cannot finish them until today, so I apologize, Miss Carter. If you would like, I can show you all the work that I completed today."

I feel uncomfortable letting people into my apartment even though I haven't been in it myself. He does have a key, so he must work here, I guess. "Sure M, that is fine. Show me what you have done. It will be like the first tour of my new home. I appreciate it." Did he just growl?

His deep voice trembles with excitement, "Right this way, bella." He unlocks the door that he had locked only moments before. "This is the living room. I had someone in here yesterday cleaning all of it, so it was completely sterilized for you. Not only did they clean the furniture, but they cleaned every room in every aspect of this apartment, even the air vents and the fridge."

The apartment was supposed to only contain a fridge, but it appeared to be fully furnished. My confusion began to bubble up to my face. I hope that rent remains the same, even if it contains more items than advertised.

I voice my concerns, "Wait, M. Are you sure all this is supposed to be in my apartment? When I signed the rental agreement, I did not remember seeing any of this; the only thing in there was the fridge. Are you sure there has not been some mistake? Maybethey put the wrong stuff in my apartment, which is supposed to go in someone else's apartment? Because honestly, with all of this, I do not think they are charging me enough rent!"

Wait, did he just look at me like I have lost my damn mind? This man completely confuses me; looking at him now, I doubt he is a simple maintenance man. What repairman do you know wears slacks and an aqua button-down to take care of an apartment?

"Miss Carter, if you do not think you are paying enough rent, you need to talk to Miss Sarah at the front desk. But

I am pretty sure you're paying enough. The furniture and everything else in here right now was from the last tenant who could not take with them. They were moving to Alaska, and it would not be logical to transport such large items. Miss Sarah just told me to leave it all here and ensure it was presentable for the next person who rented apartment A4."

Did he just lick his lips? What in the world is wrong with this man? It did it again, his eyes turned again, I am so confused! Why is my heart palpitating?

"Where did you say your second job was? Because you are not dressed to take care of an apartment. Honestly, you look like you just stepped out of a magazine... Oh, my goodness, I am so sorry. I do not know why that slipped out of my mouth!"

Why in the world would I choose to say that now? Now that was supposed to stay in my head, I feel my face turning eight shades of at least red. I am so embarrassed. M is going to avoid me like the plague. Oh my gosh! I cannot even look at him; I just focus on the floor. I need to figure out how to get him out of here quickly!

He is grinning from ear to ear, "Don't be embarrassed, Bella; I work real estate and do maintenance for this place. I have a house to go show a house as soon as I leave here. Let me show you the rest of the apartment, and then I'll be on my way."

Oh goodness, I feel like I really stepped into it!

"No worries, of course. I really don't want to make you late!"

He continued to show me around the apartment. The kitchen could be an industrial bakery. It is so gorgeous and big. My bedroom has a connecting bathroom with a bathtub that could fit the whole football team from my college. I cannot wait to get in that bed tonight! Especially since I thought I would have to put my bed together and all my furniture and stuff would not be here for months because I would have to buy it piece by piece. But I guess this is a blessing in disguise. I will not complain, but I need to talk to Miss Sarah and see if they will up my rent because this place feels out of my budget. Finally, he showed me the guest bed-room.

"M, I think there has been a mix-up. My apartment was supposed to be a one-bedroom with a half bathroom. But this feels like a palace." Never would I have imagined little ole me could afford a luxury apartment like this!

"Trust me all our rooms here are like this. The landlord of this place keeps everything in top condition, which is why it is so hard to be able to rent here cause rooms do not open often. I have been working in this building for 10 years. The boss is strict and does not let anything slide, they make sure everybody follows the rules and nobody gets away with any violations of anything. Trust me, you have nothing to worry about, here you are safe. Can I ask you a serious question?"

Oh no, here it comes. "Sure, M what's on your mind?"

"Why did you choose the fourth floor? Isn't it hard for you to make it up the stairs? I noticed you struggled to get up here, especially carrying your suitcases. Is everything all right?" Is he concerned about me?

Tell me why I did not feel like he was judging me. It felt like he was genuinely asking me if I was all right and if I was struggling.

This is weird; why do I feel at ease around him?

"Why does it look like you just killed my cat, I get asked stuff like that all the time. I chose the fourth floor for the view. I promise I am fine. This is me on a good day," I dry laugh, "If you see me on one of my bad days you may have me locked up. I struggle to walk daily; it takes me thirty percent more energy to do trivial things like walking. It is all due to my very non-hidden medical condition. I have cerebral palsy and I am not ashamed of it. I appreciate your concern M. I am not upset in any way. After I nap, I'll be good as new, especially since I just walked six and a half miles with my suitcase from campus."

There he goes again, looking at me like I lost my damn mind.

He shockingly replies, "You walked six and a half miles here with your luggage, are you insane? Not even an athlete would do that if they did not have to! Where is your car?"

I giggled, "Trust me, I am good; I do not have a car. I cannot drive due to my CP. I only have an ID and no driver's license. This is my day-to-day and how I get around." His eyes went as wide as his head. "You overexert yourself like this every day?" H says while he looks at the floor. "I do not think I overexert myself per se, but yes, this is my routine. I look at my watch, "Is it noon?!"

He finally looks up, "Yes, Bella, it's noon; why did your face turn to worry?" I throw my suitcase on the ground, pull out my black skirt and dark blue button-up, and run to the bathroom. "One second, I'll be right back!" I run into the guest bathroom, strip down, throw on my professional clothes, and open the door.

"Okay you have to show your house and have a job interview at the Ballentine office building, I need this job I've only paid two months' rent with my savings."

He looks like I just hit him in the chest. "What are you interviewing for at the forbidden Ballantine building?" Everyone at school says people call it the forbidden building because you go in as one person, and by the time you come out, you are forbidden to be the same again.

"Just an assistant to the assistant of Mr. Ballentine, I only have an associate degree, so I am limited in my options. But I am so sorry I talked your ear off about me! I want to get to know you better since I will see you here, but I must walk. My interview is at 12:45, at 12:10, and it is a ten to fifteen-minute walk for me. So, can you walk with me for the short distance downstairs? I have to get a move on. I cannot be late!"

He sighs, "Of course, Bella, let's go." He puts a blank card in my hand, and I turn it over.

It has the name Jared and a phone number: "This is the number of the best driver. He works for the car service that comes with the apartment. If you get the job for him, that way, you have a ride to and from work every day."

Now it is my turn to look at him like he has lost his damn mind! "There's no car service included with the apartment is there? I do not remember seeing anything about that!" He smirks, "It's something the landlord implemented last week. It's very new, but the tenants love it. Each floor has four dri-vers. I know Jared personally; he is always available at the drop of a hat."

"Wow, that is amazing! Okay, thank you. If I get the job, I may call him. If not, I will not. But thank you for letting me know." We finally reach the bottom of the stairs, "Good luck with your open house! This is where we part ways. I am going to speed walk to my interview. Thank you for the tour and info; see you soon, M!" I say as I speed walk as fast as my half-working legs will take me. Time to nail this interview!

2

Massimo

What is it about this girl?

She is not a girl; she's definitely a woman.

I do not understand why I am drawn to her. She is like nothing I have ever encountered. I cannot stop staring at her as she walks hastily to her interview. Little does she know she will interview at my office building for my company. But she will not get the position she applied for. I will make her a regular assistant in the accounting department. That way, at least for a while, she doesn't know I am there, but I can see her gorgeous face every day at work. I never thought I would meet someone like her who is so determined.

She is determined to change people's views of disabled individuals and two just to make her way in the world. She is a bright face in this dim and grim world. I felt like I was returning to life just listening to her speak. Ever since that cold-hearted snake broke my heart, I have never let another woman into my mind, even, but this girl has seemed to wiggle her way to my heart and my mind.

I pick up my phone and call, "Jared, I need you to be free always in the mornings and afternoons. Now, I will be sending someone here away. I need you to drive them anywhere they need to go, no matter what time of day or where they need to go. I will up your pay to $20 per hour. You think you can manage that?"

I heard Jared mumble, "You are joking, right?!" Then he cleared his throat and said, "Of course, boss! That is no problem at all. But you do not have to increase my pay that much. You know you already pay me well. Does this person you are sending my way have a name? I thought I was your personal driver."

I chuckled, "Kassani Carter, and yes, technically, you are still my personal driver. But I need you to take care of Kassani. She has trouble getting around and cannot drive. I gave her your number and may have lied, but I told her you were part of the car service, including the apartment she is renting in my building. But she doesn't know I am the landlord; she thinks I'm the maintenance man and my name is M. And I intend to keep it that way as long as I can. She seems like a sweet soul who does not care about money and doesn't need to be intertwined with the likes of me. I know this is the most we have talked about anything, Jared. But I would be grateful if you could help me keep my secret from her for at least a while. Think you can do that?"

"Dang, boss, what have you gotten into? I know the actual stuff you are into, but all this is for a girl. Are you serious? I have never seen you like this, especially after the incident with the Queen Bee. How long have you known this girl? And what makes her so different? Wait, scratch that boss. I do not need to know. Yes, I will help you, sir."

Jared is one of my most loyal employees. He works for me on the legal front and the not-so-legal front. "No worries, bother, thank you. Come pick me up outside the apartment and take me to the office, but go back to the office. I do not want to be seen."

The car starts, "Yes sir, see you in five."

I quickly text Hailey, my assistant.

"Hire Kassani Carter, but not as your assistant. Hire her as Darren's assistant." I see the typing bubble.

"Really, boss? Do you know her? Have you slept with her? Just kidding. Whatever you say."

She knows I cannot fire her, so she talks to me however she wants. I swear my little sister is going to be the death of me. "Thank you. I'll see you at dinner." She instantly replies, "Whatever, bro."

How does my sister read me like an open book? It is probably because of all the crap my father put her through. Before he died, he had signed a contract to have her married off to the capo of the Russian mob.

They were at the altar and about to make a plan to get her when I sent my men in to kill my father; why, you ask? He had hidden cameras in my sister's room where he was selling the footage of her on the illegal market. He even had a camera in her bathroom. Because of my father's actions and because my sister was being stalked, I refused to let him live. Who in their right mind would do that to their child, their flesh and blood? My men and I stand cut from a different loin cloth than my father did. Before he died, he was still trafficking women. I took care of that as well. For all the women who needed a job, I either found employment where they wished or gave them a job at one of my many businesses. Take Sarah, for example, who manages my apartment building. She was one of my father's victims. Sarah is the best manager I could ask for. After all she has been through, I am incredibly grateful to her. I ensure all the women live comfortably and never have to worry about being in a situation like that again. There were two hundred and fifty women we rescued, and all of them were under the protection of the Ballentine Bratva. That is the not-so-legal stuff we partake in. Well, it is not all bad karma that we get ourselves into. We are heads of several nonprofits.

Rather than simply firing them, I made sure to have every single one of my father's men executed. My mafia organization was created from scratch, starting with the basics. I needed men who I was sure shared the same values as my sister and me. I say men, but my mafia consists of over one thousand men and women. Some women we rescued decided to join us, because they are a huge part of keeping the trafficking out of Chicago, and Hailey is the head of them.

She may act sweet and fragile, but I have seen what she can do. After Hailey found out what her father was doing, she has not been the same, but amazingly. She cares for everyone in need of anything, but can also put any man in his place. I always try to stay off of her bad side. Haley is more intimidating than some of my capos. One capo likes to bring out her bad side: Dorian.

Hailey doesn't remember, but Dorian was beside me when we rescued all the girls that Hailey had overseas. Also, Dorian let me know what my dad was doing to Hailey. Dorian is someone I definitely could not lose to my crew. He's been there since day one, and when I say day one, he actually got hired by my dad and my dad almost killed him because he told him to his face that I would one day be a better leader than him. I will never tell Dorian, but he's my best friend and brother.

Loyal people are hard to find today, but I met Dorian in school. I have known him since we were nine years old. By the time we were 15 years old, nothing could separate us; Dorian came to live with us when we were 11 years old, right before my mother died. She was adopting Dorian when she passed. She called us her twin angels; we were born a day apart. Dorian's mother, who was killed by Dorian's father, was her best friend. No one knows why Dorian's mother was killed, and he was at a friend's house the night it happened; all I know is I will never let him cry again. I will protect him with my life.

I don't like thinking about it, but my mother was killed four short weeks later in a car accident. Part of me wants to believe it was Dad's fault, but the other part of me just wants her to be at peace. My life has never been easy, and I know there's no way out of the mafia, but I try to make the best of the cards I have been dealt. Maybe that's why I'm so drawn to Kassani. It's very weird. I've known her for less than a day, and it feels like she is in the sunshine on my dark day.

I feel as if this girl needs protecting. She may even need protection from me. But she's had a rough life; I want to learn more about it. People have been telling me it's time to find my purpose because they don't suspect what I do for a living. They think I'm the lowly maintenance man at my apartment building. It definitely has its perks; I have four cops that live in my apartment building. I don't mind being mistaken for help. It makes me feel needed. Kassani hasn't been needed much in her lifespan. Part of me wants to give her everything she's never had and ensure that the world does not treat her as it has been. Soon, I will find out everything; I will have Dorian run a background check and find out everything he can about her. As a Bravta leader, I know how cruel people can be. But from this day forward, I will not allow anyone or anything to dim her brightness.

It is a little funny that someone as bright and shiny as Kassani caught my eye when I thrived in the darkness; I was my best self after dark. Darkness is my haven; I feel like the real bad happens during the day and the calm only comes at night. Most nights, I stay at the office until 7:30, then head to the apartments to see if any work needs to be done. Most nights, I don't make it home until 9:30 or 10:00, depending on how much I get caught up doing.

After I leave the apartments, I usually head to Dorian's place. We go over everything that we need to accomplish for the next day. Making it home, Hailey updates me on how all the girls are doing and lets me know if there's anything I need to be concerned about regarding any of the charities. I don't make it to bed until 12 am, sometimes 3:00 AM. I have never needed to change my routine; no matter what I do at night, it always speaks to me. I can't believe it, but there's this unknown part of me that wants to be seen, that may even not shine. If I believed in God, I would say it was his plan, but I believe I'm not worth saving. But there are many people out there who are worth saving, and I intend to save as many as I can, even if it's just by doing the little things that they need me to do, like making sure they have food and shelter. Crime is inevitable in every town, but at least I can control it in this town. No one else is as powerful as the Ballentine Bratva.

Four mafias, if you could call them that, have tried to overthrow my reign. Each one of them learned quickly that I get what needs to be done, but it's not just me you need to fear, it's the surrounding people. Haley, Dorian, and even Jared are all my secret weapons.

Hailey is good with small weapons and her legs; I will never spar with her again. She almost broke my back just by squeezing it with her legs. Dorian's weapon of choice is a 22 Beretta, which he secretly calls Hailey and thinks no one knows. But I remember reading it in his diary when he got it at the age 16.

Jared is good at everything, but his favorite thing to do is snipe. You give that boy any rifle and a target just know that, target he's probably not going to make it, he has only missed once since I've known him. I have known Jared for 15 years; arson is his specialty, the sniping is just his hobby. No one messes with my people. Not even me. Everyone wonders what my specialty is. I don't have a favorite. I prefer not to use violence unless I have to. The world already has too much violence and death in it. I don't want to add to it unless it's absolutely necessary.

I slowly crept into the back door of my office building to reach the security room and watch Kassani's interview. When I finally saw her, she was shaking hands with Hailey. Tonight, I'm going to ask Hailey her honest opinion of her. I slowly turned up the volume and listened to my girls talk.

"Welcome to Ballentine Industries! Your resume was impeccable, Ms. Carter. Both of your references had nothing but glowing reviews of you. We have a few questions for you. Are you ready to begin?" Hailey smirks.

"Of course, I'll be glad to answer questions you may have. What would you like to know?" Kassiani looks at Hailey with confidence and admiration.

"What is your greatest asset for a job? And how do you handle tough situations?" Hailey should have stuck with the usual questions. I have no idea where she's going with this.

Kassani takes a deep breath and replies, "My greatest asset to the great workforce is my time management and dedication to anything I'm working on. As for tough situations, I deal with tough situations all day, every day. Right now, I don't know what I would do without them. They're difficult to maneuver, but nothing is ever out of my control. I guess you can say I've become an expert on handling tough situations."

Why do I feel that Kassani feels comfortable around Hailey? Hailey is a natural mother figure—at least, that's what all the girls say. I think Kassiani handled that very well. Most people don't know what to make of Hailey.

"That was definitely not the answer I was expecting, but I love to see that you are a great time manager and are dedicated to everything you do. I'm sorry you deal with many tough situations, but trust me, your expertise will serve you well here. I rarely do this, but I would like to offer you the job. When would you be able to start? And have you decided on a salary range?" I need to let Hailey do all the interviews.

Kassani stutters, "Um...Sorry, I hadn't considered it yet. I know that with my last job on campus, secretarial work, they paid me $12.00 an hour; could we talk about going higher than that? Would that work?"

Has she lost her damn mind?

There is no way I would pay anybody in my company that little.

But let's just see how this plays out. I'm sure Halley's going to do the right thing.

"OK, that's a good starting point; I will talk it up with the higher-ups and get back to you in the morning. Would that be OK? I'm sure that's not going to be a problem. Thank you for coming in. You are just a delight. You are exactly what we need in this company. I will see you tomorrow morning at 8:30."

Hailey played that off and was calm and collected. She knows as well as I know that is not what I will be paying her.

"Thank you so much. I appreciate this opportunity! I will not let anybody in this company down. Yes, I will be here bright and early at 8:30 in the morning!" Kassani enthusiastically replies. I can't wait for her journey, our journey. This looks to me like the start of something new. This way I will keep an eye on her and ensure she gets everything she wants and needs, as well as ensure nobody messes with what is mine.

3

Kassani

I can hardly believe it—I'm still in shock!

When I walked into that building, I had no idea I would get hired on the spot.

Everyone had warned me about its terrible reputation, filling me with a mix of apprehension and curiosity.

However, as I stepped through the doors, I felt an unexpected thrill coursing through me. It's an exhilarating opportunity! I can't wait to begin this new chapter in my life. For the first time in a while, I'll be able to send money back to my family, something I've longed to do. I'll do whatever it takes to support them because their well-being means everything to me.

Tomorrow is my first day, so I think I will take a quick shopping trip; tomorrow calls for a new outfit. I have a little money to spare, so I can at least get myself a new shirt and skirt for tomorrow. I want to make the best impression I can on my first day.

Growing up, I was never allowed to go shopping, not because I didn't want to, but because we never had the funds to afford new things. Growing up, we struggled, we struggled month to month and check to check. I saw how hard my dad always worked; my mother worked too and you could see she was getting tired of the same old job. Never in a million years would I imagine that the home I knew would become a broken home after I left home. As I went off to college, things at home got intense; my little brother would message me telling me about the bad days. But no matter what, I would always keep encouraging him because I didn't want him to suffer, and I wanted him to make it through school and be the best he could be.

Turns out little did we know that our parents have been on the rocks for years. They finally decided they no longer wanted to be together due to some interesting circumstances. But sometimes I think that my brother and I are better at it. I know for a fact that my dad is different, and by different, I mean completely happy. He has been completely happy since he started over; he remarried at a very intimate four-person ceremony. Which I was lucky enough to attend. He and Celeste got married on a frigid day in December.

They are an example of when life tells you who your person is, to run and jump, do anything you can to find and keep them. My dad and Celeste have no care in the world now because they are not struggling, and they come home to a house full of love and laughter instead of regret and fighting.

I strive to one day have a relationship like they do. Because love is rare these days, everyone is more concerned with lust and scratching an itch instead of what it takes to commit yourself to one person. I've been the victim of men just wanting to date me because I fall in a different category than every other woman because of my medical condition. Meaning most of the time, they see me for my disability and not for me. Men have just come up to me and wanted to take me on a date just to see what it was like to date a physically disabled person. It's very debilitating knowing that people don't see me they see my handicap.

Maybe one day I'll be able to find a man who accepts me for me and is more worried about me than about my condition, and maybe I can get lucky and find someone who can accept both and see me as a bit of a normal person. I have been told many times that love is not possible for me. That I am just a burden to society. That no one in their right mind could fall in love with someone who needs extra care and extra help all the time. What they didn't know is that I don't need extra help and extra care. I do a good job taking care of myself.

I've been away from home and at university for the last five years. I was not put here to be a burden on society. God created me in his image and as my best self. He wanted the world to see that everyone is different, but no matter what the circumstance, kindness is the key to survival. Everywhere I go, I am kind to everyone because everyone is never kind to me.

One day, I want to be seen in the eyes of the world as making a difference or even merely existing. I don't want to stand out just because of my condition. I would rather blend into the background and have no one know that I'm there. If my family would just feel like they didn't have to protect me or care for me as much, I would be happy. I feel like they worry for me because of what I go through, but I just want them to be the best they can be and thrive in this world. That's why I helped them in any way I could; I am the oldest of all my siblings. We could make an entire basketball team if you add us all up. A family shouldn't have to struggle just because I was built a little differently, so making up for that in any way is my duty.

Every day, I think about my last relationship, which lasted almost two years. He did a number on me. He made me feel unimportant, unloved, and very self-conscious. He made it seem as if I could not do anything without him or his permission. Living with him was like being locked in a prison, 24/7, not able to make your own decisions about what you eat, what you wear, and how you act. There were times when I almost slipped back into my negative ways and ended up dead.

All because the warden was too self-conscious about being with a physically disabled person. He always negatively commented about my hair and weight while talking to supermodels on social media. But it grew into him using his fists or anything he could handle. Makeup was my best friend for almost a whole year. But after two years, they finally had enough and told me I would never amount to anything and no one would ever care for me the way they did. Little did he know I was content alone; what if I ever wanted another relationship again? I would find the right person first. They will have to go through a lot of vetting. I'm not up for dating jerks or men with control issues. If they want to control me, they better not even come near me. I'm a new person.

This new me doesn't stand for control, and I know my worth, so I had better be treated like a princess or something close to it. But if they can treat me like that, I can treat them like a king because Dad ensured I had all the skills I needed to make a man succumb to my charms.

My dad taught me how to cook, clean, and do laundry, which has made me very self-sufficient—unlike many women my age. I rely solely on myself for everything I need to do each day. As long as I can get out of bed and handle my responsibilities, I won't depend on anyone else. That's why I'm feeling uneasy about the situation with M.

I don't understand why he makes me feel like I need him. I just met him, yet it feels like we've known each other for years. I've never had a connection with anyone like this before—not even with the jerk I was with for two years. I'm very independent, and I don't want to lose that, but maybe I would consider it for M.

What am I thinking? I cannot let a man affect me this way! I must have lost my mind.

I need to focus on myself and doing what I came here to do, which is provide for myself and my family. I cannot let anything get in the way of my goals. I will hate myself if I let anything stop me from becoming the best person and providing my family with the best life possible.

Why can I not get M out of my head?

What is it about him that draws me in? Oh my gosh, Kay, snap out of it!

I need to focus; I need to focus on finding a cute outfit for tomorrow. First impressions are everything in the professional world. I can't believe I let my thoughts wander.

It took me 30 minutes to get to the store. I needed to hurry up and shop before it got dark so I could walk home while it was still daylight. OK, so what kind of outfit am I looking for tomorrow? I need something classy and elegant but also professional and easy to move in. And possibly something that does not show off my legs. I don't like people staring at my legs with how I walk.

Okay, first we'll look for a skirt, then if I don't find any options that are long enough, I will go with pants.

I enter the store and look around; I feel like I don't belong there, but I will not let them know I feel out of place.

It is very high class. Two chandeliers are hanging from the ceiling. All the workers are dressed to the nines with heels and jewelry. But the store's appearance will not offend me; they aren't staring yet, so that's a good sign. I'm just going to make my way over here where I see these skirts and dresses and find something I like. As I make my way over to that section, I now notice the employees start to stare and whisper.

Here we go again. I have a feeling that either they're going to say I should not shop here, or they're not going to stop being up my ass until I leave. I'm not worried about them. I'm just going to mind my own business and do what I came to do. I don't see any skirts that I like, but these royal blue pants are my absolute favorite. Royal blue is my go-to color for everything in my closet. Royal blue is my safe color. I feel like when I am wearing royal blue, not as many people stare or comment on how I walk. I guess you can call royal blue my haven. I picked up the pants and read the size, and they were a perfect size 22. Because I'm a little on the bigger side, but again my size does not stop me, nothing does. As I'm eyeing the pants, I see the employee start to walk towards me. She looks a little timid, like she doesn't want to talk to me, but let's see how this goes.

"Excuse me, ma'am, do you need help finding things? Or possibly finding a new store to shop in?" I look at her name tag. On her name tag it says Karen is her name. I take a deep breath, smile at her, and prepare myself for what's coming.

"Thank you so much, Miss Karen. I'm perfectly fine. Thank you so much for asking. I like these pants, so I think I'm going to purchase them, and that'll be all I need today. Thank you so much for your concern."

She honestly looks flabbergasted at my response. She looks me up and down before she replies.

"OK, a little advice. Next time, shop at a store that caters to outcasts."

She proceeded to ring me up, and that was the end of that; that is a basic example of what I go through every day.

People these days have no regrets for shaming mobility-impaired individuals.

4

Massimo

It has been one month since Kassani started working for me.

I have had Jared watch her anytime he has a chance.

She wasn't kidding; people treated her like a second-class citizen. Just because of how she walks doesn't mean she should be treated differently than anyone else.

Anytime, Jared, please let me know if she's been mistreated or talked down to. If I have an account with that place, I will withdraw it, and I'll ask Jared to suggest another option for Kassani. Everyone in the office loves her. I have never met anyone as sweet as she is. I often refer to her as my sweetheart and my Bella. We have gone out a few times, but she still doesn't really know who I am; I need to tell her soon before my feelings for her continue to grow. Putting her as

Darren's assistant was my best decision; she has never seen me in the office. It's surprising because she talks to Hailey and eats lunch with her every day.

I did a little research into her background over this past month. I also have her medical history in a separate file. I might need to read that later to know how to care for my sweetheart properly. Little did I know that her childhood best friend, Kiera Madison, works for me. Kiera has worked for me for almost 5 years now.

Kiera is an assistant and one of our biggest volunteers at the soup kitchen as we run. Kiera had a hard upbringing. Maybe that's why she and Kassani bonded so much. They grew up in the same small town, and it turns out they have the same birthday, December 12. From what I found, both of their moms were best friends. But then they both got married and went their separate ways, which didn't make it easier on Kassani and Kiera.

From what I found, the girls were close until Kassani moved. Looks like Kassani had been bouncing back and forth between two towns since she was in kindergarten, and then her parents finally decided to stay in a little town just outside of Chicago so she could finish school without constantly moving. Kiera was heartbroken. They did everything together; they had been having birthday parties since they were two. When Kassani's parents found that it was time for them to stay and not move back again, the girls were in sixth grade, but in ninth grade, both started struggling.

I only know all this because it's a public record. Kiera was in and out of juvie because she was always getting into fights and feeling alone because the only person who really understood her was over 2000 miles away. Kassani was in and out of mental health facilities, as she had always had Kiera by her side to make her feel confident. Kiera never let anything happen to her, and Kassani was never bullied or treated differently when Kiera was around. Kassani had to learn to stand by herself and not let the world get her down. Phone records show they have had brief contact through-out the years. They have just been texting now and then. It seems that no matter what; they are there to support each other despite the distance between them. Kiera missed what happened a few years ago with Kassani's mother and father. Hopefully, she can help my sweetheart through it better. I don't know much about it except they divorced a few years ago.

The girls don't know that they work in the same building. I know Kiera's routine because she is engaged to Marco Ballentine, my cousin who runs the soup kitchen and some of our other legal businesses. So, I will have Hailey cancel lunch with Kassani, so she has to eat in the employee cafeteria on the eighth floor.

Kassiani

Well, there's been a change of plans.

Usually, I have lunch with Hailey on the sixth floor where her office is located. However, she had a very important meeting today, so she had to cancel our lunch plans. Hailey and I have become quite close over the past month. We talk every day and sometimes even text each other after work. As a result, today I'll be heading up to the eighth floor to have lunch in the employee cafeteria. I've heard that Tuesdays are the best days to eat there because they offer a full restaurant-style menu. I think I'll treat myself to some Ragu pasta. It's been my favorite since childhood.

My best friend Kiera and I used to indulge in it whenever we visited my Nana's house.

That was unexpected. It's amazing how that just popped into my mind. It's been almost 2 years since I last heard from Kiera; I really should check up on her soon.

As I step into the elevator, my thoughts consume me.

My childhood wasn't the easiest, but that's to be expected when you're seen as an outcast in society.

However, Kiera was my rock. She helped me through it all, and without her, I wouldn't have come this far. We were inseparable. We were even born on the same day, in the same hospital, in neighboring rooms. It wasn't until later that we discovered our mothers knew each other, but that's a story for another time. Kiera was my protector. She never allowed anyone or anything to harm me.

When my parents broke the news that we were moving permanently, I was devastated. I knew that my life would never be the same again. I had to learn how to rely solely on myself without any safety net. It definitely had a profound impact on me throughout middle school and high school, as I became a target for bullying every single day. Mentally, I was in a really dark place, and it eventually reached a point where I attempted to take my life. To put it simply, the guys at school singled me out as an easy target for bullying and harassment, and they went to great lengths to try to exploit me. This is a story that spans a considerable length of time, with numerous details and complexities.

I finally reached the eighth floor of pasta heaven. Here I come! In a month's time, I have come to love my job. I never thought I would like to be someone's assistant. But I'm making enough money to put money back and help the people who mean the most to me. It has its perks if you eat in the cafeteria; it is completely free, and any leftovers they have, they don't throw out and give to the soup kitchen. I found out that the CEO of this company actually runs it. After all the bad things I've heard about this place, it looks like they are doing well, as well as their community, which makes a little old outcast me feel wonderful. This world needs some good in it.

As I approached my table, I noticed a very familiar face. This cannot be happening right now!! Why are all these good things happening to me right now? Only Kiera Madison was sitting at a table right next to where I was going to sit.

I could not believe my eyes. We are actually in the same town and working in the same place.

I am so grateful that I got this job. I will check in with her and see how she's doing.

"Kiera? Is that you?"

Kiera looks at me, does a double take, and engulfs me with her signature hug.

"No way in hell! Kassani, are you kidding? Tell me this is not a dream. Are you really here? It's been two and a half years since we've seen and talked to each other, right?" I giggle. It feels like no time has passed between us whatsoever. We are back to acting as we have always acted with each other.

"It's me here. I am in the flesh! Can you please slowly release me so I don't fall?" I joke. "How have you been, Key? I've really missed you." Oops, I probably shouldn't have used my old nickname for her.

"Kay, this has just become the best day ever!" she says, jumping up and down with me still attached. "Oops, sorry, Kay! I'll let go! I'm so much better now; you just made my entire year! Do you work here? Where have you been hiding? Where are you staying? Do you need me to bring you anywhere? Where's Dad? How's the family? We have to catch up. I have too many questions!"

It's good to see she hasn't changed one bit. I didn't realize how much I really missed her until I saw her. "Key slow down. We do have a lot to catch up on. And it's not all good, but it's not bad either. Do you have any plans after work? We can go to the sandwich shop down the street and catch up. I cannot believe we work in the same place; miracles do happen."

Key puts her hand on top of mine. "Yes, of course. I'm free after work today and tomorrow. I spend most of my time volunteering at the soup kitchen now when I'm off. Time needs to hurry up, Kay! I cannot wait to catch up with you. We have been apart way too long. What floor do you work on?"

I smile. "I work on the sixth floor."

"Have you met Hailey, the devil's assistant? She is so sweet and wonderful; I don't understand how she puts up with the devil!" Kiera replies.

That is interesting. Some things I have heard about the CEO could be true. Let's see what else we can find out.

I shrug, "The Devil? Really Key? Have you met him? There's no room for another devil in my life."

She gasps, "Oh Kay! I am so sorry! I forgot about that. You always used to call him that. Is he still around?"

I sigh. "It's a long story that I promise to tell you after work. That is not something I want many people to know about."

Key pats my hand. "I understand. I can't wait to hear everything tonight! Sorry to dine and dash, but my lunch is over. I work on the seventh floor, but I'll meet you on the sixth floor, and we can go to the sandwich shop together."

We hugged, and she was off. I still can't believe that my backbone is in the same town as me. Can this day get any better? Just as I think, my phone vibrates in my hand. It's a message from M.

It reads, "R U FREE ANY THIS WEEK?"

He has not learned to text without shouting; I giggle and then reply.

"Only if there's ice cream involved."

He responds immediately, "DEAL! TOMORROW AT 6?"

I smile and reply, "Deal, but I'm buying."

I put my phone in my pocket and headed back to work. Life right now is sweet for me.

5

Massimo

This woman never ceases to surprise me.

She really thinks I am going to let her pay for our date.

Some people may know my reputation, but my Bella doesn't. I refuse to treat her any less than a queen. She has gone through enough trials and tribulations to last a lifetime, so if I can help it, no more worries or struggles for her as long as I am breathing. I don't think I have ever felt like this. I can't go for a few days without finding an excuse to see her.

Just last week I went to her apartment to see her, and I found some interesting details about my sweetheart. First, she asked Sarah to raise her rent because she felt guilty about the free furniture. I have already informed Sarah that this is not going to happen. Secondly, my doll has no idea how much she gets paid at my company.

My little sweetheart thinks she's only getting paid a little over $12 an hour to do this job. Does she know our minimum pay at my company is $40 an hour?

She opted to go paperless so she doesn't really see how much she makes. Anytime I'm with her I make sure she's not paying because I know $40 here in Chicago is the low end. I'm getting excited about our date. I'm hoping we can soon start dating for real, and she will agree to be mine. Little does she know what being mine entails. She's in for the wild and spoiled ride. I want her to understand that not every man is there to take advantage of her, men like me just want to take care of her. In this cruel and unusual world, I may be one of the bosses of this crime town, but I have a soft side that hasn't come out of me in years. From what I've learned, Kassani does not deserve to be treated as an insignificant being; she is one of the treasures of this world.

My ex did a number on me. She was cheating with some of my dad's old recruits before I had a chance to kill them off. Her name is Rosalie Angelo. She is the daughter of the third-largest crime family in the world. Her father is Roscoe Angelo, who used to be my father's greatest ally. Till everything came out about what Dad did. A few of Dad's allies were on his side, but Roscoe was not. That is the only reason he is still living. Rosalie, not only was she caught cheating, but she was caught giving our enemies information not just my enemies, but her fathers, too. I heard a recording that one of my men made when he was spying on her for me. She stated that the only reason she was with me was to get information so she could have me killed. Because she wanted to take over my Bratva. That is not going to happen as long as I still live.

After her, my love life has been almost nonexistent. There has been the occasional hook-up here and there. When I dip my toes into the world of women, it's just women who work at one of my clubs downtown. Until a month ago, that's when my cold and icy heart finally started to thaw. Kassanni is my sunshine to this gray world. Even my men have been commenting on how much I've been smiling. Little do they know, all my sweetheart, I have done is hug and a few cheek kisses. For a man like me, it has taken a ton of restraint not to go further with her.

I could see us waking up to each other every morning in my king-size bed and eating breakfast at my 12-foot dining table. I would not mind cooking for my sweetheart ever, cooking has been my hobby since I was younger. It was the main thing me and my mother did, even after her death I couldn't bring myself to stop cooking. It's a way for me to escape all my bad thoughts and clear my mind. If my men knew this side of me what would they think?

I am the leader of the Ballentine Bratva.

I have killed two hundred and forty people since I've been in power. I am a killer, I am a monster, I am the epitome of the Grim Reaper.

Death for this city is in my hands and my hands alone.

No one will see my soft side, no one but my doll.

Hopefully, she never learns about the monster I've come to be known as in the town.

Kassani

What are the odds?

How in the world did I end up in the same town as Key? We have been apart for 5 1/2 years, but it feels like we haven't been a part at all. Conversations between us are still as easy as ever. Kiara is the only person who's fully understood me.

There is so much we have to catch up on. I want to know what's happened these past 5 1/2 years. The last time I knew, her mom had shipped her off to boarding school because she felt like a more structured environment would benefit her. Her mom didn't like who she started hanging around. This made no sense because the last time Key told me she was hanging out with our old crew, Somehow, we had a group of geniuses that didn't look at me or treat me any differently. There were six of us in total in our group. Maybe one day we will all meet up again.

As I make my way back to the sixth floor all that is running through my head is my past. Looking at me now not a lot of people could tell the struggles that I've gone through. When I was 14 life became too much for me, I tried to end my life. I got very lucky because I had a very patient and concerned teacher who watched me like a hawk. They got me to help. I needed it right away, and I haven't tried to end it since. But that all happened because I let one boy, yes, a boy because we were teenagers, treat me like I was nothing, and made me feel like if I was no longer here, nothing else would matter. I was so low that I felt like I wouldn't be missed, and I would just be taking care of another burden on society. He was the one that I used to refer to as the devil. But recently he reached out to me.

He contacted me through my social media and had a lot to say. When we were younger, he treated me as an object. He treated me like I was just there as a benefit to him, not as an intelligent young lady. He would take and take from me, both emotionally and physically. It seemed to be the main thing he was concerned about, even as a teenager, was just sex. Later in the line, I found out he chose me only due to a dare with his group of friends. We dated for two years through middle and high school, looking back I don't know how I allowed myself to be taken advantage of. But when he contacted me all he wanted to do was apologize. He said karma had come around full circle and he had been treated the way he treated me. He told me he fell in love with a woman who was only with him for his money.

Of course, I accepted his apology. I have learned that very few grudges benefit you in the long run. He definitely deserved closure and to be happy without any guilt. After that, he didn't contact me again, which is fine. I hope everyone in my past is able to move on and thrive.

Sitting back at my desk, I open all my agendas for today. The only things I have left for today's meeting are to take notes for Darren in today's meeting, then get them edited and sent out to the team. The meeting is in about ten minutes. I let Hannah know that I was heading to the conference room for the meeting, she is Darren's head assistant. She waved and smiled and I was on my way. It was hard to believe that everyone here is so lovely and accommodating. I don't feel like people are judging me, and I don't even feel like an outsider.

As I step into the conference room I grab a seat in the furthest corner I can, I don't want any attention on me. As I get settled people start to trickle in. Familiar faces greet me, just the coworkers I see daily. Then in comes Hailey, smiling and looking like a supermodel in her Gucci dress suit. One day I will be able to afford something nice after my family is settled, they are my main priority.

There are rumors that the big boss is in the building, the monster that owns the building and signs all of our paychecks. Everyone always refers to him as the monster. His legal name is Massimo Ballentine, if you google him you will not find a single picture. When I googled him, I found a few pictures of Hailey, which threw me in a loop.

Is she a Ballentine? I just thought she was his assistant. Is she his lover? Rumor around the office is that she is a VIP. Now, I need to figure out how it correlates.

The last of the employees started to file in. looks like the meetings are fixing to start. I wonder who's leading the meeting today? I like meeting new people in the office, hopefully, one day I can have work friends. my eyes are still fixated on the door, in walks Key I didn't know she would be at this meeting she smiles at me and sits right down. My eyes drift back to the door; standing in the doorway is a tall, broad figure I did not think I would see at the office.

He clearly doesn't notice me, which is fine. I'm buried behind about 15 people in this big conference room.

What is M doing at this company?

Is this one of the other jobs he was talking about?

I'm a little confused.

Hopefully, he will give me some insight into what's going on.

He starts to introduce himself, and my heart drops.

"I am Massimo, CEO and founder of Ballentine Industries. I have met most of you. But I do see some new faces in the room. Thanks for joining me today to review some new company policies. Today, we will discuss the pay rate change for all departments and the new schedule for the design department. All right, let's get started. I will not waste your time so you can return to your duties."

His face drops as his eyes meet mine. I guess he's realized the cat's out of the bag.

Honestly, I don't know how to feel right now. I'm not trying to stand out in this world. When dating the CEO of Ballentine Industries, what will people think? I'm a nobody who barely fits in this world. Why would he choose me? I found myself starting to have a panic attack. Breathe In. Breathe Out. Breathe in, breathe out. Do not freak out; you don't need to draw attention to yourself with all these people around you. Okay, the breathing helped. Unfortunately, I tuned out of the meeting after M started talking, I mean Mr Ballentine. Why me, why choose a woman who has expressed that you just want to be normal to be with when you are one of the most infamous people in the entire world? all the rumors that go around about you I don't know how to decipher them, good Lord why me?

Finally the meeting comes to a close, I let everybody file out before me before I even attempt to leave. Part of me is still in shock. Is the CEO of the company I work for my boyfriend? Do I know the real M? How long has he been hiding this from me? He's not a maintenance man? This definitely explains why he fights me about paying for things. Why would you be with someone like me? As everyone files out it's just the two of us left in the conference room.

I quietly talk to him with my eyes on the floor, "Good morning sir. How are you doing today, Mr. Ballentine? I'm very shocked to see you here. I thought you said you were in real estate, or was this the big real estate you were talking about? Was any of it real? I really thought I was starting to feel something for you."

Not once did I bring myself to look at him, but part of me felt like the biggest fool.

It feels like I made the same mistake again, letting a man use me.

Massimo

I am panicking!

How was this an oversight?

My sweetheart was not supposed to be at this meeting. She is not the lead assistant.

Why was she here? She was not supposed to find out this soon.

We just started getting close to building our relationship.

She won't even look at me, keeping her eyes to the floor. She looks a little heartbroken. How am I going to explain this to her?

"Kassani, sweetheart, I'm sorry. I did not want you to find out this way. Please look at me."

Her gazes snapped to mine, "How did you want me to find out, sir? We are in my place of employment; don't call me sweetheart!"

Her anger is evident in her tone.

I have never seen her upset.

As soon as she was done speaking, her eyes went right back to being glued to the floor. I must keep my cool and not let my Bratva side come out; she is not ready.

"I understand. I will explain this to you in detail later today when we are not in the workplace. Whatever you do, please do not shut me out. It was not my intention to hurt you. I promise you I will give you all the answers you seek."

She huffs, "Sorry boss, no time for you today. I already made plans, that don't include you."

Damn where did that fire come from, I like it!

"That is quite alright, I will explain everything to you. Are you free tomorrow?"

I lift her chin with my finger.

"I'll have to check with my boss. I hear he's a real tyrant."

Was she joking and flirting with me while mad at me? The little sweetheart is feisty.

She might be the perfect fit in my world. She is not your typical spitfire, but I can see that no one can walk over her once she opens up. I imagine all my men will love her, but not like I do.

Yes, I admit I am in love with my sweetheart, but she will not find out just yet.

I let a hardy chuckle slip, "I hear he is a real pain in the ass. But I am sure I can convince him to work around your schedule. Does after work tomorrow work for you? I would like to show you my house."

When she sees my house, I'll be able to gauge how she will handle the rest.

She takes a deep breath, "Yes sir, I think I can squeeze you in. Send me the address and I'll walk there after work."

"Okay, sweetheart. I promise it's not far from you. I am closer than you think. You overdo it too much. Relax, sweetheart. Let me help you. I promise I'm not trying to buy you."

I lift her chin again. She will learn to look at me.

She is a strong, powerful woman. She needs to reign; she needs to be free of whatever is keeping her down.

She snapped her head out of my finger, "Touch me without my permission again and you will not like what happens to the finger of yours. I will hear you out sir, but on my terms only. Give Jared your address, he will take me there tomorrow after work. But he will be outside waiting for me, I will pay him. That way if I don't like any of what you have to say I will leave with or without your permission. I have shown you the sweet and caring side of me, now it's time you feel my wrath when it is deserved. See you tomorrow sir. You wasted enough of my workday. I must get these notes sent out as soon as possible. Good day jerk whole I mean sir."

With that, she gracefully stomps out of the conference room, looking back only to glare at me.

What the hell just happened?

Where did that sass come from? That's the Kassani I need, the strong and feisty queen.

I hope she accepts me.

I don't want to lose her.

She's not only my sweetheart; I can see her as my queen.

6

Kassani

Who does this man think he is?

He can't order me around, outside of work, that is.

I don't know how to wrap my head around this.

Am I dating my boss?

Am I involved with the man who there are so many rumors about you can't tell the difference between fact and fiction?

What rumors could be true?

What rumors are fake?

Does he sell women? Too many people have been saying that he's part of a woman trafficking ring. That is possible for him to be a cold-blooded killer. The side, I know is sweet and loving and always looking out for me, but was all that a lie just to get what he wants?

Part of me thinks it's not a lie because he hasn't gotten anything from me. He's just been spending time with me and making me feel special.

But another part of me is scared out of my mind.

Did I make another big mistake? Is this man using me for his gain?

What would he have to gain from a broke and handi-capped woman? Why do I fall into traps like this?

What is it about me that makes me look like easy prey? I feel like part of my heart has been ripped out of my chest, and I am starting to love him. He's shown me what it's like to be cared for and feel like I matter. But I can't dwell on it, I'm just gonna get through the rest of this workday and then meet up with Kiera.

Especially after today, I need some girl time. Hopefully, everything between us is still the same even though it's been years since we last saw each other. I just spoke with her a lit-tle bit. I felt right back at ease, like we were in high school.

She's always been my strength.

As I get these notes sent out to the company, I can only think about M's and my interactions. It's weighing on my mind. Finally done. Finally got all the notes typed out. Send a company-wide email now, concluding my workday right on the dot. As I gather up my things, I can't help but wonder if maybe M had something to do with me getting this position. He wouldn't do, would he? Just stop it, Kassani. You have all your answers tomorrow. You just need to relax and enjoy time with your friends. As I finished packing up my purse, she was there. Kiera's always had this grace about her, anytime she walks into a room. She can command attention if she wants to, but if she doesn't, she won't. She's tall and graceful and always well put together. I strive to be like her one day.

"Hey Kay, are you ready to go?" She smiles and I'm already at ease.

I grin, "After today's events I am ready to run!"

" A lot of us saw that confrontation in the conference room. Is everything OK?" Key asked worriedly.

"It's a crazy story that I promise I will tell you. But I want to hear about you first. I've been apart from you for too long. Don't spare any details and please tell me everything! Especially if it deals with your love life!" I reply as enthusiastically as I can muster.

Key is blushing! I don't think I have ever seen her blush.

"Key, you better spill it right now!!!!"

Now I'm emotionally invested again. Thank goodness I can forget about my problems for a while.

She takes a deep breath as her blush grows. "So I've been in a relationship for two and a half years now. He, um, how do I say this? He's related to Mr. Ballentine, his cousin Marco. Marco saved me from a very serious situation."

I now see the fear in her eyes.

"What kind of situation? Are you alright?"

My heart breaks for her. She went through a ton of stuff in high school. She deserves nothing but good, whatever happens. I know she didn't deserve it.

She gulps, "I was in the process of being sold as a sex slave. Marco was undercover for someone and happened to buy me to save me. He and Massimo got me back on my feet, they paid for my medical bills and my house. If it weren't for them I wouldn't be alive today."

What the hell?! How did someone so pure get wrapped up in something so disgusting?

Tears spring to my eyes, "Key honey, I'm so sorry! You shouldn't have gone through that. I'm never leaving your side again! You've always been the strong one out of us, but let me be strong for you. I will not let anything ever come between us again, not even a man! I'm sorry I wasn't there for you; from now on, it will be like the old days. If you don't reply to my call or text, I will be at your house before you know it! I will never let you down again."

My tears just keep flowing. I'm crying for Key and myself. After all these years, life has just now started to look up for us. Why do we deserve to go through all these tribulations? We have done nothing but good in this world!

I feel Key's arm slide around my shoulders, "Don't cry for me, I'm safe now. It only happened because I was blinded by love. My ex-fiancee sold me to cover his gambling debt. I know what mistakes I made, and those will never be re-peated. Besides, Marco would never allow anything to hap-pen to me, he is my salvation. Massimo had a big hand in my rescue too, don't worry about me I have tons of macho men watching over me. Tell me what happened with you and Massimo."

Just as my tears stop, I feel them resurfacing, I start to shake.

"My house is right down the road, Key. Will you walk there with me? I am not comfortable talking here."

She nods and helps me up, and we go to my apartment.

As we approach my building, Kay brushes my arm with hers and asks, "Kay, you live here? You do know who owns the building, right?"

My heart rate starts to pick up, "No, I was told it was someone who barely shows up at the building. Why are you looking at me like that? Do you know something? Tell me, tell me now!"

Key is looking at me like the cat is stuck in the bag.

"Um, well, it has something to do with our boss." She can't look at me as we get to the elevator. "Kay, how much do you know about Massimo? Like what details of his life do you know?"

I sigh, "Well, for one, I just found out his real name today, and for two, I didn't know he was my boss until today either. So apparently nothing I know about Massimo is correct! I just thought I could have a normal relationship for once. I just thought that I finally found a man who doesn't look at me like I'm broken and a burden! But maybe I was just a charity case to a man with more rumors around him than the quarterback! The worst part is my dumb ass was falling for him."

As I finish my rant, the elevator opens on my floor.

We walk to my door, six feet from the elevator.

There is a sense of recognition in Key's eyes.

She places her hand on my head like when we were younger; we called it the sister pat.

"Kay, sit down. I am probably not supposed to say anything about this, but I have to because we've been friends since birth. Just promise me you will talk to Massimo tomorrow, okay?"

I sit on the couch and look up at her. "You know something huge, don't you?! Fine, I promise. You never make me promise unless it's big or life-changing."

"Kay, don't shoot the messenger. Let me tell you a few things, and we will go from there. Nod if you understand." I nodded; she knows me very well. I couldn't speak because she could see I was already in panic mode.

"I used to live in this apartment a year and a half ago after the incident. All this furniture is here because I wanted a certain look for my new home, and the landlord said it was fine to leave it because I know him personally. Honey Massimo owns this building."

She sits beside me on the couch sensing that I am about to lash out.

Breathe in, breathe out, in, and out.

Nope, it's not working.

I jump up from the couch, "You have got to be shitting me right now! Next, you'll tell me Jared works for Massimo, not the apartment complex!"

She giggles and pats my head.

"Yes, honey, that's the case. Jared is like Marco. They work together. But that information will not be coming from me. You will have to talk to him. I have already told you way too much." Key hugs me, trying to keep me calm. "Calm down. You don't want to have a seizure. You know what happens when you get too stressed."

"Yes, Mother, I know I'm calming down. But do you know Massimo's address? I will not wait until the morning!"

Key laughs, "That won't be a problem, honey. The whole top floor is his. You can only get to it with a special key that you put in the elevator. I have one of those keys just in case.

I'll give it to you for the night. Don't do anything I wouldn't do."

I hug her neck, "This is why you are my Key! Key with the key!"

Massimo

Please tell me why I see my voluptuous brown-haired, blue-eyed beauty bang her fist on my door.

No one comes up here ever. I love the serenity and the peace.

Who gave her a key to my floor? She is still pissed. You can feel the heat radiating out of her pores.

I have a feeling she found out some other details about me, and she just can't wait to wrap her sensual arms around me. Oh, who am I kidding? This woman looks like she wants to murder me.

I swing open the door with all my might. Then I lounge sexily, "Long time no see, sweetheart. What can I do for you at this fine hour?"

Sassy ass pushes me back into my apartment, "Cut the shit. I need to know everything and don't leave anything out. Who knows who comes up here? We are not talking in the hall. You better start talking your sexy head off."

She huffs as she finishes her sentence and plops on my couch; she looks worn down and emotionally exhausted.

I did this to her. I made her so drained.

Is she all right, both mentally and physically?

What does this mean for her health?

Is she pushing herself too far today?

It was never my intention to harm my sweetheart.

I take a deep, calming breath and reply, "What do you want to know, sweetheart? I am your open book. Throw your worst at me. I think I can take your tiny rain shower."

Oh shit, looks like I awakened the beast. Her eyes suddenly changed from sky blue to abyss black.

Damn, my sweetheart can move. In less than ten seconds, she got up from the couch and pushed me into my leather recliner.

She didn't hesitate; let's see how long it takes her to realize she is in the recliner with me straddling my lap.

I feel my dick starting to stand at attention; this woman gets to me in every way.

My hands slide to her hips as she snaps, "Tiny! I will show you a tiny rain shower. I just want to slam my tiny fist into your face! Just tell me the truth M....I mean Mr. Balentine."

My sassy sweetheart is hardcore blushing, she is as read as a tomato.

I feel her breath hitch, and maybe she's realizing the position she just put herself in.

She keeps looking me up and down. She's staring at the deep of my shirt, I only had the last three buttons buttoned. She's slowly caressing my chest. I slowly rubbed my hands up and down from her hips to right underneath her breasts. She only squirms a little. Her sweet little hand makes it to the top of my waistband.

She jumps off my lap, "I apologize, sir. That won't happen again. My lines are so blurred right now. it's going to take me some time to adjust to the fact that you are my boss and not the man I'm dating."

She says she looks at the floor, I see maybe a hint of heartbreak in her eyes.

"Sweetheart, you can blur any lines you want. This is exactly why I did not want you to know who I was. You were getting to know me and not what everybody else sees. If you'll have me, I will continue to be the man you are dating. But I promise to explain everything and keep nothing from you. Tell me what you know sweetheart. I know Kiera must've said something."

I slowly walk towards her, place my hands on her waist, and tilt her chin to look at me.

No queen should ever look at the floor.

She stumbles backward, I gently bring her back to me. "Sir, I'm sorry. Kiera didn't tell me much, just that she's dating your cousin and that you and he saved her from the trafficking situation. She also told me you own this building, so it seems you're not M, the maintenance man, but Massimo, the landlord. Most of all, Mr. Ballentine, you're someone everyone in the office thinks highly of, but you also think you might be part of the mafia. So that's all I know, would you care to clarify Mr. Big Bad Wolf?"

I swear, this woman and her sass!

I just want to kiss her and tie her to my bed so she can get the rest she needs, but also if she will allow it to show how a queen should be treated. "Drop the formalities, sweetheart. I'm still your M. But let me ease your mind. I'm not part of the mafia; I'm head of the Ballentine Bratva. I do some illegitimate things sometimes, but that's on a need-to-know basis. But my company, Ballentine Industry, is completely legitimate. I also oversee a few charities here in Chicago, and yes, me and Marco saved Kiera from some sex trafficking, but we also saved all of the women involved and gave them a new start with jobs and homes. Marco was taken with Kiera, so she got special attention. I'm glad that they are both happy and thriving. Sweetheart, yes, I'm your boss, but I want a relationship with you and to show you how a queen is treated. Some people may call it spoiling but I call it showing a woman their value. I have feelings for you, so would you please give me a chance? I promise I will tell you anything that you want to know, even if it is illegitimate. What do you say?"

After all that her eyes go right back to the floor, I will show Kassani her worth.

Kassani

I push myself away from Massimo.

Can he read my mind?

Does he really want to treat me like a queen?

"Give me a minute. I can't think with your hands on me."

I walk to stand in front of the massive window that stretches the length of the apartment.

As I stare at all the people walking in front of the building, I feel myself shutting down. He is part of the Bratva! I thought that was only something you read in books about.

Is he a murderer?

What are all the illegitimate things that he does?

Does the good he's done outweigh the bad?

What game is he playing?

Why me?

Why a broke, handicapped girl?

What can he gain from me?

Am I being used again? He saved Keira, he can't be all bad, right?

Where do we go from here? Do I continue a relationship with him?

I'm getting dizzy.

My head is throbbing, and my heart is palpitating.

Oh no, I feel like I'm about to fall, my muscles are giving out. I back up just enough so I can lean on the couch. I will not faint.

I will not panic. Breathe, Kassani, don't let him see you at your weakest.

You haven't had a seizure in almost three years, push through you know your body.

I steady myself and breathe some more making sure I am relaxed and not stressed.

"Well, um, I am very shocked. I appreciate you telling me everything, but what are you playing at? Why me? You can have any woman in the world and probably someone who's already a part of your world. I feel like you are still hiding something from me. Be honest with me, please, and quit playing with my emotions. I've been through too much already in life to be lied to."

Massimo slowly approaches me. "Can I touch you?"

I nod. He strategically places his hands on my hips. "I recently found out someone you know works for me. I didn't make the connection until I reviewed his background check again."

What!

Who could I possibly know that it is a part of the Bravta?!

"I don't know anyone who would be involved in this! Who do you think I know?"

He pulls me closer to him and places his hands on my shoulders. "Does the name Roman Hart ring a bell? He's in his twenties."

What! Did he just say what I think he said?

"Who did you just say? Repeat the name because there is no way!"

I gaze up at him, and my hurt is apparent.

Massimo pulls me in close, "Sweetheart, Roman Hart, your brother works for me."

That's the last thing I hear before my body gives up on me.

My body starts shaking, my head thrashing and throbbing.

I can't form words, and the shaking won't stop.

The last thing I see is my M looking scared out of his mind.

My mind goes dark, my eyes shut, my limbs fall limp, and all the while, I'm sweating profusely.

After four years, the streak is over.

7

Massimo

I barely caught her before she plummeted to the ground.

What is happening?

She can't hear me calling her name, she is not responding to anything, and her body is completely limp. I hit the emergency button on my smartwatch, and Jared's voice answered instantly.

"Yes, boss? How can I help?" Thank goodness he was still outside!

"Start the car; we must get Kassani to the emergency room immediately!"

I am panicking. Could I be losing her right now? How often does this happen, and what happens?

I go down the back elevator so we don't cause a mass panic in the apartment building. Jared helps me get her in the car. I told him not to worry about the speed limit; we must get there safely.

Kassani is laid across my lap in the back seat of Jared's car.

I will not let anything happen to her.

I swiftly texted Roman and Kiera to let them know and to have them come to the hospital.

Am I about to lose my sweetheart?

Did I cause this? Has this happened before?

As we arrive at the hospital, Jared opens the car door and I rush to get Kassani seen.

"Somebody help, please! She's been passed out for 15 minutes now! She collapsed in my arms! I don't know what to do! Please save her!"

All eyes are on me with a heartbreaking sadness, but one nurse rushes over.

"Mr. Ballentine, we will be glad to help bring her into this room. I will get the doctor on call. Do you know her medical history?"

How could I not have looked at her medical history after everything she told me?

It's still unopened on my desk!!

I reply, "She has cerebral palsy. But that's all she's told me."

The nurse gives me a weak smile, "Okay, that's a good start. Give me her details and I'll see what I can find. Also, if you have her phone details, they might also be in there."

As I look for her phone I hear a familiar voice behind me.

"Her name is Kassani Carter. She is 28 years old. She has cerebral palsy, with a history of seizures. Her last seizure before now was 4 years ago. She's allergic to all pain medication except tramadol." He puts his hand on my shoulder, as the nurse runs to get the doctor.
"Thank you for coming, Roman. You must've been close. I'm sorry, but this is how our next meet-up is happening." I lower my head to the ground.

"Please, sir, don't beat yourself up. You didn't know. I was already on my way to see her. One of the boys heard you run her background check, and I popped up. I knew it was time to come clean with her. Boss, how long have you been seeing my sister? Please spare me the intimate details."Roman sits down beside me, keeping his hand on my shoulder.

I chuckled, "Noted. We have been spending time together and getting to know each other for a month. So I guess you can say we have been dating for a month. I have never met anyone like Kassani. For your information, I respect your sister so much that I won't make the first move. We are taking this at her pace. She told me a little about her past; I don't want to repeat any of those mistakes. She deserves the world, she deserves to reign! If she wants to be my queen, she will reign!"

He looks at me astoundingly, "Boss, where's beast I and boys know and quake at the sight of?"

I snicker, "I am still here. Your sister brings out the best in me since we have been getting close. I still do my job, and so no mercy when it's required. But if I don't have to be inhospitable, I won't be. She has done a number on me in this short time." I put my head in my hands. I feel defeated, I need her to wake up.

The doctor finally enters the room; I am instantly at ease because I see it's Doctor Sara Rossi. Sara is one of our success stories, she was kidnapped and almost sold into the trafficking ring. We made it just as a thug was trying to beat her into submission. After we saved her we made sure she could finish medical school after she had worked so hard.

She pats my shoulder before evaluating Kassani.

"Massimo, what's going on? The nurse told me her history. What exactly happened?" I recount the whole ordeal to her, minus the details of what I did, because Sarah said if it's unnecessary, keep her out of the Bratva loop.

"Understood, we will get her vitals and send her for a CT scan. It sounds to me like she had a seizure. If that's the case we will give her fluids and make sure her body and brain are not harmed in any way. We will figure this out! I will be right back with the nurse to get her going. Massimo, I am her friend as well, please let me know if you need anything." Sara pats my back and rushes to get the nurse.

I turned to Roman, "How many seizures has she had that you know of? How bad were they? What should I expect?"

Roman walks over and sits in the chair across the room and runs his fingers through his hair, "This is the first time she has had a serious seizure in the past four years. The last time she had one was when she went through a breakup with whom she used to call the devil. But last time we spoke, she said he reached out and forgave him."

He sighs deeply and looks me dead in the eye, "How serious are you about her boss? I'll tell you everything if you'll be with her for the long haul, but I must know if this is real!"

As Roman finishes speaking, Doctor Sara and the nurse enter. "All right, boys! We are taking her for testing. She's in good hands. We will be back in a few minutes. Get some food and coffee. When you get back, I'll update you both." I nod at Doctor Sara, then Roman and I walk down to the cafeteria.

I clasp my hand around Roman's shoulder,
"You don't have to worry friend. I'm not going anywhere unless Kassani tells me to pack my shit and go. How did someone so special fall into our world?"

He guides me to an isolated bench right outside the cafeteria. "Buckle boss, I know Kassani would leave some parts out of her past, but you deserve to know the whole story. I believe you, I think you have fallen off a cliff for my sister. So, are you ready?"

I feel like a weight has been lifted off me.

I reply, "Yes, brother, I'm ready."

He takes a deep breath, "Kass is damaged. Her CP is from violence; her biological father shook her when she was a baby and caused a lack of oxygen to her brain. Before you even suggest it, no he's not dead because Kass forgave him and would not want it that way." He runs his hand over his face and continues, "She was bullied all through school because of how she walked and talked. She tried to end her life twice, but luckily I was there the second time or she would be gone. Now she is this bright and shining star who tries to make everyone happy. The men she's dated have treated her like scum, and I made sure that was handled. Now, her main priority is taking care of Dad and our siblings, and she's not doing that alone. Our dad remarried and Kass and Celeste are thick as thieves, they talk almost daily. But the main reason she is so emotionally drained is because of the number her mom did on us. She cheated on Dad and then decided she would only contact us when she wanted to. The worst part is Kass forgave her, then she left and still hasn't come back. Thats her biggest fear is people disappearing from her life. I have to text her every day just to ease her mind."

He stands up, "With her medical condition she needs someone who will not stress her out and will keep her sane. But most of all put her first. Boss, do you think you can handle that? If not she can leave with me."

Did he just try to threaten me? No, he wouldn't do that, he's been loyal for 5 1/2 years. My poor sweetheart has been dealt a shitty pile of cards. Who in their right mind would abandon her and treat her like scum?

I rest my head in my hands and reply, "Roman, I will protect her with my life. She will suffer no more, and I will not allow anyone to put her down or stand in her way. I see her as my forever."

I slowly gaze up at him as he replies, "Boss, you're under Cupid's spell." He pats me on the back and chuckles. "Let's go check on Kass boss."

We go back to sweetheart's room and hear giggles and tears coming from there.

Kiera sits beside Kassani in her bed, holding and tickling her. You can see the love in their eyes for each other. Kiera's tears keep streaming, looking like tears of relief.

No one should be able to hold her right now but me! Calm down, M! That's her best friend; no jealousy is needed.

At that moment, Doctor Sara arrives, "So glad you're awake, Kassani. So it was like I suspected, you were passed out for so long because you did have a major seizure. A migraine caused the seizure this time. It's a condition called Migralepsy when migraines trigger seizures. In rare cases, it can be major; other times, it can be light. There's no treatment for it, but limit your stress and take care of yourself and yourself, and you will be fine."

Before I could say anything, Kiera said, "Doctor, could over-exertion of her muscles and mind cause this?"

Doctor Sara nods, "Most definitely! Kassani, are you prone to over-exerting yourself?"

Kassani's lips form like she's ready to say no, but before she can, all three of us must respond, "YES!"

Kassani crosses her arms over her chest and sticks out her lip like she's pouting.

Sarah clears her throat and responds, "Well, since the answer is yes, don't overexert yourself for at least two weeks. I'm sure these three will keep you in line. Remember, take it easy for the next few weeks. I don't want to see you back here anytime soon. Just sign these papers, Ms. Carter, and we can't get the nurse to remove your IV, and we can send you on your way." Sara hands Kassani the papers.

Kassani hesitates before signing the papers and asks, "I am cleared to return to work tomorrow, right, doctor?"

Sara doesn't even get to answer before the three of us declare, "NO!"

Sara retorts, "I think your three nurses have the right idea. There will be no work for at least three days, but the rest is up to these three. You are in excellent hands, Ms. Carter."

The actual nurse removed her IV, and we headed to the car within minutes.

You can tell Kassani is feeling better because as we walk to Jared's car she snaps, "You three nurses, get in the car now!! We are heading to pick up sushi, and we will all have a long chat at my place! No one is exempt!"

Roman says, "You had me at sushi, sis. But you must promise to sit down and take it easy while we talk or we are leaving, deal Kass?"

She hugs him and replies, "Fine Roe, I promise. Now let's go I'm famished!"

What the queen wants the queen gets.

8

Kassani

When I woke up in the hospital, I was grateful; for once, I didn't want to die.

Kiera is back in my life, and Roman came to see me! They are my two favorite people in the world.

I am not mad at Roman for hiding that he's part of the Ballentine Bratva; I know he was trying to protect me. Those two have been there in my darkest moments. Then there's the boss man, the new addition.

What do I do? Was he trying to protect me from his world, too? Can he be the one to take care of me? Would I fit by his side? Would I hold him back? What would be expected of me? Will he learn to love me? Can he handle my condition? What is in store for us if we go head-first into this relationship?

I have to get out of my head! I need to take it one day at a time. I'm alive; that's what matters. I have at least a small group of people who care about me. I don't feel my mind slipping into the abyss anymore; I feel like the clouds are lifted. Could Massimo be my sunshine?

We finally arrived at the sushi place.

I placed and paid for a big order of California Rolls because three of us could eat the entire order. But I knew the boss man wouldn't eat any of it because he doesn't like seafood, so I ordered the biggest chicken fried rice and orange chicken I could get.

Hailey was kind enough to let it slip out one day at lunch that the boss didn't like seafood, but of course, I was blind to the fact it was M.

Roman returns with the order and smirks, "Sis, overboard much?"

I giggle, "Nope, Roe, I'm just prepared! I know how much at least three of us eat when we get together, so I ordered the usual amount and then something for Massimo—something without fish."

M looks at me like a lost puppy, "How did you know that? I have never said anything."

I bat my eyelashes,""I have my sources, boss man""

As we make the final stretch to my apartment, I stare at M. He has never been this silent; he has a stoic expression.

Is the man contemplating life or writing his will? I really don't know. He looks sad and lost in thought, he hasn't even noticed me staring.

Everyone files out of Jared's vehicle.

I grab one of the rolls from Roe's trays and hand it to Jared. I sweetly tell him, "Thank you for getting me safely to the hospital today, and thank you for putting up with me every day."

He nods and mouths, "Thank you."

As I spin around my foot gets caught on the pavement. Oh shit! I just got out of the hospital, and I'm about to land myself right back there, or so I thought. It was like a movie seen. One minute, I almost fell to the ground, and the next minute, I fell into the arms of a 6 foot 2 inch brown-eyed Zeus!

The grace that this God catches me with! It's like he spins so that I could lay perfectly against his rock-hard chest. Swoon! Oh goodness, I'm so cheesy!! Kass, gather your thoughts, don't open your mouth, and look like a numb skull!!

Those sexy, deep, and lustful brown eyes are pulling me in! My hand lays perfectly on his bulky peck, and oh my, his scent is intoxicating!

Lower your head, M kiss me, boss man! Oh, screw this. He is as stiff as a board, scared to touch me. Not on my watch big man!

I slowly caress his face and lower it to me. He tries to slow me down, making me want him more. I yank his lips to mine and I swear I see fireworks! His lips are like heaven, oh and that tongue is a playful hell! We only break apart when I hear Roe clear his throat.

Roe snarkily comments, "Do Key and I need to leave now?"

I swivel around in M's arms, where my ass is against his crouch, and move his hands to my stomach and slowly reply, "No, little bro let's go eat! I want to spend time with all of you."

As Roe and the others turn and make their way into the apartment complex, I wiggle my ass against Massimo's trousers.

I rub his legs and say, "You better fix that boner, boss man." I kiss him again and make my way to my fourth-floor apartment. I can feel his eyes on my ass, I look back at him as he adjusts his dick.

I chuckle and tell him, "I'll boss you now, and you can boss me later."

I guess my heart has made up its mind. This man owns me, I may never be the same again.

Massimo

What the hell?!

Kassani kissed me!

It wasn't some sweet and tame peck either!!

She grabbed my face and pulled me to her soft and sensual lips, and made me forget my surroundings!

She instantly intoxicated me!

She manhandled my face! She wanted me!

If only I could read her heart, maybe there are feelings on her side, too. I love her; I need to protect her.

I want to teach her the ways of the Bratva and make her strong and unstoppable!

Why in the world would she rub her luscious ass against me?

It was so hard not to touch her right out in the open! She could have made me submit with just a wiggle. Is she a witch? Because I was indeed under her spell!

Kassani really has become the light to my darkness.

I need to stop thinking like a love-sick puppy. I am the Don of the Ballentine Bratva; I must start acting like it! If I show her my dark side, will she still want me? What could this mean for us?

We all make it up to her apartment and file in. Kassani makes us comfortable in the living room to eat and spend time together. When this will be a silent dinner the doorbell rings.

Kassani jumps up and answers the door. I hear myself scolding her, "Slow down! You're supposed to take it easy!"

She glances over her shoulder at me and retorts, "Calm down, boss man. I'm just answering the door, don't get your panties in a bunch!"

I growl and go back to eating, I see Roman and Kiera giggling and I give them the finger.

Marco was at the door, he nodded in my direction as he leaned down to kiss Kiera.

Kassani claps her hands, "Now that the whole group is here, who wants to fill me in on the Bratva life? How about you, little brother?"

Roman choked slightly on his sushi, "So that's how it's going to be, Kass?!" He clears his throat. "Well, I started working for Massimo when you went off to college because I knew you would try to handle the family's financial responsibilities independently. I met Marco shortly after they rescued Key. I oversee the protection and daily operations for Massimo charity Operation Hope. Operation Hope caters to anyone who needs assistance with housing or dietary needs, and this charity helps keep people off the street. So I'm mainly working on the legal side of the Bratva unless I am instructed otherwise."

Roman goes right back to eating. Good man! He gives her all the pertinent information without lying to her. I have only involved Roman in one inhospitable situation, and that was helping take care of the thugs who harmed Kiera and too many other women. But sweetheart doesn't need that information.

My sweetheart sighs, "Okay, bro. Thank you for being honest. Don't forget I know all your giveaways when you are lying." She then winks at him.

Oh my, she is a smart and sassy little thing. She quickly glances at me and then turns her attention to Marco. "Marco, how long have you worked with the boss man? And what are your intentions with Key? I may not be as rich as you, but I know how to make someone suffer."

Marco starts coughing, as Kiera starts laughing. After Marco gathered himself, he said, "Officially, I've worked with him since 2010. But I've been by his side since we were 15. He's my best friend and family. As for Kiera, I'm in it for the long haul. We are already engaged but intend to marry in a few months. I don't hide any of what I do from her, especially since she went through the ordeal. She is amazing and she helps so many people. But most of all she makes me a better man." Kiera rests her head on his shoulder and interlocks her fingers with his.

You can see the love and respect radiating from each of them. Maybe I'll have something like that one day.

Kassani

Well, today has been an emotional day. I ended up in the hospital and found out I had a new condition, and I found out that my little brother works for the Bratva!

But my best friend is back in my life, and she's engaged and madly in love with her fiancé, who also happens to be part of the Bravta. But maybe one day I'll fall in love like she has.

Right now, I care about Massimo deeply and strangely don't mind that the rumors are true. He's the Don of the Bravta and may have possibly killed people. But from what they have told me, I'm unsure if they do more good than bad.

I know he does so much good in this city, but it's time to find out from himself. I heard everyone else's side.

I adjust my posture, look him dead in the eye, and say, "So, boss man, tell me what you're in charge of. I'm waiting."

He smirks, "Sweetheart, I'm in charge of everything. We have been successful because of how we all work together! My men matter to me. I'm a cold-blooded killer, I know how to clean up any mess I make. Nobody, and I mean nobody, can harm anything or anyone close to me. Why you ask? Because baby I have eyes all over this town. Let me put you at ease, sweetheart; all the rumors are true. The good ones and the bad ones. What else do you want to know?"

Did he really say all that? The animosity behind that was unnecessary.

Is he trying to scare me off?

What the hell is his problem?

I get ready to respond when Roman stands up.

"Kass, I have to get to bed. I have to be up early in the morning. Boss, is it okay if I crash at the clubhouse?" Roman hugs me, and Massimo just nods. It's like there's a hidden meaning there. I will figure it out.

Marco and Kiera rise too. Key hugs me and whispers, "Give him hell, Kay. Call me in the morning."

What is that supposed to mean? I'm confused. But then she crosses her fingers, puts them on her forehead, kisses them, and puts them on her chest. She just did our sign from sixth grade!! It's how we say, "Be smart, love hard, and die trying." Marco smiles and just smiles; he knows. I do it right back, with my fingers by my side, ending the end to say, "Always."

I shut and locked the door. As I turned around, I lean against the door and said, "Just so we're clear, the only place you can boss me is at work, boss man."

9

Massimo

This woman is trying to provoke me.

I see the lust in her eyes.

She is saying everything she can to get a reaction out of me. Little does she know I'm the king of manipulation; she's not going to like it, but she will obey me.

I slowly inch closer to her. When I reach the doors, I place my hands above her head. I bring my lips as close as I can to hers without touching them and say, "I am the boss of this entire city, don't you forget that, sweetheart. Which means I am your boss by default."

I caress her cheek slowly, bring her lips to mine, and place a chaste kiss on her lips.

Then I pick her up, throw her over my shoulder, and chuckle, "It's bedtime for you, princess. You had a very exhausting day, so you are confined to this apartment for five days. While I am at work, Roman will be here off and on to look out for you, and Jared will be here as well, so if you need something, give him a ring."

As I put her down at the entrance to her bedroom, she snapped, "Have you lost your mind? You don't manhandle me like that! You are not allowed to touch me without my consent! Next time, my tiny fist will be in your face! And I am not staying here for five days. I have work to do."

I push a strand of hair behind her ear. "Your boss said you're on sick leave starting now. Everyone gets sick leave from the day they start. And sweetheart, you forget I own the building. Everyone will follow my direction if I say you're not going anywhere. Get ready for bed. If you're not tired, we can watch a movie. But if you're tired, let me know, and I'll be right here in the guest bedroom."

My sweetheart huffs and puffs turns around to get ready for bed, and whispers, "Whatever, jerk whole."

She will eventually realize I am only doing what is best for her. One day, I will show her how bossy I can be.

Kassani

This man is a real jerk whole!

He acts like he's attracted to me, and then the next I know, he is toting me off to bed!

You have to be kidding!

Is he trying to look out for me, or is he trying to torture me?

I definitely care for Massimo, but do I care for this over-protective attitude? Yeah, actually, I do. No one besides Roman, Kiera, and my dad has protected me. Could this be the man who was made for me?

When I look at him I don't see just a man. I see a crown floating above his head, and fire radiating from his eyes when he looks at me. He never makes me feel incapable, but he makes me feel unstoppable. He knows how to handle my sass, and he showed today he knows how to keep my ass in line. I have never felt like this. Is this what it feels like to be cherished?

I'm going to spend some time with Massimo tonight. I want to see the desire in his eyes, to see him look at me like I can do no wrong. As I look at my reflection in the bathroom mirror, my voice of doubt returns. It's the voice that almost ended my life.

It says, "You are not worthy of his power! He deserves someone whole. Fix your walk, fix your weight! No king wants a princess with a cracked crown by his side!"

I need to get out of my head; I know I can be worthy and will be worthy one day. I cannot allow the negative effects of my past stop me from living and finding out where this can go with Massimo.

I need a distraction.

I jump in the shower and do a quick scrub to wash all the hospital gunk off of me.

I pick my shortest and silkiest pajamas in my safe color, royal blue.

Let's see if this king can resist this princess.

Massimo

When I heard the shower turn on, I knew she would want to stay up. I cleaned up the living room while Kassani showered.

Keira, Roman, and Kassani really ate all the sushi they had.

Who eats that much sushi?

Kassani ordered me way too much rice, Marco, and I couldn't even make a dent.

Does she realize what she is doing to me? She is driving me insane! Can she see how much I want her? But given to-day's events, I will not take advantage of her. She deserves the world; how could anyone treat her any less than she treats the world?! She is like an angel sent to Earth to save us; after COVID, we need saving. The world is still nowhere near where it used to be.

The crime we have been dealing with lately is getting out of hand. Our biggest problem right now is a rival, Bravta, is trying to bring drugs and trafficking into our city.

My brothers have been researching it intensely with all of our resources. I can tolerate drugs only to a certain point, but trafficking I will not stand for!

Marco, Roman, and I will be there to take them down.

No more women deserve to get hurt. Marco says Kiera still has nightmares that cause her to scream in her sleep if the room is too dark.

Marco said Kiera mentioned how Kassani used to sleep but didn't give me details.

It makes me wonder how she would look asleep.

What would it be like to lay beside her and hold her all night?

Which side of the bed does she prefer?

What is her bedtime routine?

What does she wear to bed?

My sweetheart comes out to the living room, freshly showered.

Damn girl, where have you been hiding that figure? Her two-piece royal blue pajama set hugs her in all the right places. An hourglass, pure perfection. Her arms look as soft as a blanket; her hips look like they belong in my hands!

M, stop drooling over her! Boundaries, she had a traumatic day! Think with your brain and not your dick!

I can't help it! I can't believe she's been hiding all those curves underneath her work clothes! Her body is faultless! Why is she so timid about her body? If you are not looking for it, you will not notice a slight difference in the muscle mass of her right and left leg. That must be why she limps. But that takes nothing away from her radiance.

I clear my throat, "You want to watch a movie with me, sweetheart?"

She looks me in the eye and replies, "How about we make a movie instead?"

What did she just say?! "Sweetheart, explain to me what you mean."

If I say more without explaining, I will end up taking things way too far. Let her be in charge. Oh, sweetheart, I'll let you boss me!

10

Kassani

Does he need me to spell it out for him?

He is a brilliant man. Is he playing coy?

Or is he letting me take control?

His eyes just changed color.

He's either frustrated or turned on.

Let's hope it's the second option. I know if he lets me, I will boss him around.

I stroll towards him, "Come on, boss man. Could you show me how bossy you can be? I am at your discretion."

When I reach him, I caress his cheek and play with his stubble. His silky black shirt already has two buttons undone, so I caress his cloud-soft curly chest hair. I slide my hands along his pecs.

Then I start flicking the buttons open.

Finally, my hands reach his waist, and I slowly untuck his shirt.

This man radiates sexiness.

Never have I been this comfortable sexually.

Massimo makes me want to be a different woman; he gives me confidence.

I started this tonight. I am determined to finish it; I reach for his belt buckle.

He gapes and takes a step back. "Sweetheart, stop and think. You just got out of the hospital a few hours ago. Do you really think this is a good idea?"

He intertwined his fingers with mine; I get he's trying to protect me, but is he really rejecting me right now?

"Boss man, I know my body. I am fine." I remove my fingers from his and sigh, continuing, "Tell me the truth! Do you want me? Are you attracted to me? I'm an adult. I can handle anything you have to say."

He actually looks hurt. He moves forward instantly and grips my hips like they are his lifeline.

"Sweetheart, I am completely attracted to you. Kassani listen to me. I want you, I am not those assholes from your past. I want you more than I have ever wanted anyone. This is not me turning you down. I ask you to give your body time to heal and adjust to what occurred today."

Massimo caresses my check; how is this sweet man a Don?

Does his men see this side of him?

He lifts my chin and places both hands on my cheeks. One moment, he looks at me like I'm breakable, and the next minute, his luscious lips come crashing down on mine. My eyes drift close; he smells like sandalwood and vanilla. His tongue finds mine and intertwines like there is no to-morrow.

His hands caress my cheeks, and then he slowly navigates them around the map of my body. His hands move from my cheeks to my shoulders, and suddenly, he stops. He stares at me like he can see into my soul.

He grips my hand and moves it to his crotch, and grunts, "Never doubt that I am attracted to you. My dick is hard as a rock, I want to rock your world. But I won't do it tonight. I want you to recover so I can show you how bossy I can be. Now, do you want to watch a movie, sweetheart?"

I feel my face turning as red as a tomato. He put my hand on his dick!

I feel like a damn teenager, I'm over here blushing like a virgin.

What the fuck just happened?

One minute, I'm in control, and the next, he has snatched control from me and turned me into a scolded schoolgirl!

I feel myself steady my breathing, and I nod and say, "Fine, bossman, you win this time! But we are watching The Notebook, no if and or butts!"

I snatch his face, crash my lips to his, and intertwine my tongue just like he did. Then I drag M to the couch and say, "You don't have to be my protector, but thank you."

As I put the movie on, he replies, "I always protect what is mine."

That's the last thing I hear before I drift off to sleep at my favorite part of the Notebook.

Massimo

Not even halfway into the movie, she's passed out. Her head started on my shoulder, and now, she's a sleeping beauty across my lap after she shifted in her sleep. As the movie ended, I let her dream on my lap for another 30 minutes, then I toted the beauty to her bed. She looks too good to be true. Her sweet, child-like demeanor is what hides her trauma.

I noticed a few peculiar things about her space as I entered her room. First, she has three nightlights on in her bedroom. Three nightlights in a 400-square-foot room seems a little excessive, but there's got to be a story there. I did notice that there were nightlights all around the apartment.

What could that mean?

Then I noticed that the bathroom and closet have their own nightlights, but the bathroom is shut and locked, while the closet is only shut.

But there were six pillows on the floor in the closet, like they were put there on purpose. The final thing I noticed was the knife sticking out from underneath her pillow.

Who broke my sweetheart?

We will have a heart-to-heart, and I need to know everything. But if she doesn't tell me I still have the report, maybe I can get to the bottom of it from there.

Looking at my sweetheart sleeping, I decided I was not leaving tonight. I texted Jared to let him know to pick me up in the morning. I will just rest in the guest room because it's closer to her than the couch.

What happened to her besides what Roman told me? There has to be more to it!

But all of that is irrelevant to what I really want—my Queen, and that's who she will be!

She has admitted that she wants me, so she is now mine!

What was she thinking, trying to seduce me tonight?

I want that more than anything, but I must look out for her well-being.

She has had a rough life, but no more! I will train her and mold her into a Bravta Queen!

I can see my sweetheart working side by side with Hailey, both being strong and courageous women.

She needs someone to look out for her who can make her reign!

I will be her king.

She will reign and rule with power and confidence!

11

Kassani

When the sun hit my face the next morning, I woke up.

How did I sleep through the night?

I haven't slept through the night in three years.

I tried to roll over so I could get up, but something had me locked in place.

As I turned my gaze to my side, I noticed a powerful bicep, its muscles bulging, wrapped around me like a firm embrace.

What the hell did we do last night?

I stop and think; I am almost positive I fell asleep during the Notebook.

I'm not sore, so we didn't have sex; why did my mind go there?!

Why is M in my bed?

I slowly try to maneuver my body away from his; then, suddenly, I'm yanked back into a rock-solid chest.

His sexy, sleepy voice says, "Sweetheart, you can't run for me; you're right where I want you."

Uh excuse me, why is my heart fluttering?

Why do I find his tone of voice a turn-on?

He could definitely boss me around right now; I mean, why not? We are already in my bedroom!

Snap the hell out of it, Kay! Find out why he's in your bed!

"Boss man, why are you in my bed wrapped around me? Release me you ape!"

I ask while pounding his bicep.

He releases me and chuckles, "Don't worry sweetheart. I'm only here because you were thrashing and flailing in your sleep. I could only get you to stop by putting my arms around you. We need to talk about that, Bella."

He stopped my tremors.

How is that possible?

I have had them since I was a child.

No wonder I slept so late and soundly, by the third round of tremors I am awake and can't go back to sleep.

I take a deep breath, "Why do you want to know? Did I only thrash once, and stopped after you held me?"

He rubs my arm to comfort me and says, "Yes, sweetheart. You slept through the night with my arms around you; you didn't flinch. Get dressed, and I'll make breakfast, then we will talk. I want to know everything about you so we can grow our relationship. Take your time. I'll be in the kitchen."

He places a kiss on my forehead and leaves me to my thoughts.

A whole night of sleep?

With a man beside me?

What world have I stepped into?

My ex wouldn't even hold me or calm me down; if I woke him up, he kicked me out of bed.

Does my body feel safe and protected with M?

What's so different about him?

This is a new experience for me. It's like I actually matter. I feel like I could be unstoppable with a man like M by my side. But ever I explain the tremors and everything else, he may not want me. But if that's the case, I will recover.

I refuse to let a man break me.

Massimo

As I make it to the kitchen, I text Jared to let him know that I'm not going to the office today, and I let Hailey know, too.

There's no way I'm leaving Kassani after last night.

Her thrashing was like she was fighting someone off in her sleep.

As soon as I calmed her down, it was like nothing had ever happened. She slept like a baby. Every time I moved, she would inch back towards me. I hope she tells me everything. I want to save her. She deserves the world.

Let's make breakfast.

She has a fully stocked fridge—omelets it is!

I put my masterpiece together, I grab the eggs, tomatoes, mushrooms, bell peppers, ham, and cheese.

I hope she likes it. I found some oranges on the counter and made her some fresh-squeezed juice. If she will let me, I will cook her every meal.

As she exits her room and enters the kitchen, I've never seen a more perfect creature. Her royal blue sweatsuit makes her look like an in-charge princess; she only needs a crown.

"Foods ready, sweetheart! Are you hungry?"

There she goes again, staring at the floor; I must fix this.

She nods as I set a plate in front of her. As she begins to eat, you can see some of her reservations melt away. So food is one way to her heart, noted.

When she finishes, she looks up at me with sad but thankful eyes and says, "Thank you, M. I haven't had a good breakfast in so long. You're a man of many talents." A small smile crosses her lips, and her eyes slip back down.

I caress her cheek and tilt her head up. "I am glad you liked it. Cooking has been my favorite hobby since my mom taught me when I was young. Sweetheart, let's go to the couch to learn everything about each other. I have a few questions for you, but I will not judge you, okay?"

She gets up, grabs our plates to put them in the sink, and turns to lean against them, "But boss man, you have to go to work."

I slide my arms around her waist and reply, "Not today, sweetheart, I'm all yours today."

I grip her hand and lead her to the couch. As we sit down, she starts to fidget. I grab her legs and place them on my lap, and she calms instantly. I rub her legs and say, "Ready to answer a few questions, princess?"

She takes a deep breath. "Yes, boss man. Just please be paid with me. I have a feeling about what you want to know; this will be tough for me."

I stroke her hair, "No worries, princess. Just take it slow, ok?" She nods, and I continue, "What's with all the nightlights in the apartment and the pillows on the floor in the closet?"

She gasps, "You noticed that?"

I just nod so she can continue, "As silly as it is to say this, I am afraid of the dark. When I was younger, I was left alone a lot in the dark, so I kept the nightlights so I always had a source of light and didn't panic. As for the pillows, the main place I was left alone was locked in the closet for hours with nothing. No pillow, no light, no food and they would be gone for hours at a time. So now, just in case that ever happens, I have pillows and supplies in the closet. See, I'm fully broken. There's too much baggage here for you to be with me."

Her eyes slip back down to stare at my hand on her knee. Who in their right mind tormented her like this as a child?

I push a stray strand of hair behind her ear, "Sweetheart, who did that to you? Does Roman know?"

You can see the tears forming in her eyes, "No, M, he can't know. It was someone who is no longer in my life, I forgave them. They are the reason I have CP. I hope one day they can forgive themselves, too. It's the past, so it doesn't matter. Roman has enough on his plate and already worries about me too much."

The reason she has CP? I remember what Roman said, so her biological father did this to her!

Where was her mother?

Who allows their children to be abused like this?

I start stroking her leg again, "Kass, you need to tell Roman. I know he knows that your biological father gave you CP, but he should know the rest. You forgiving him shows how mature you are. I will never let anything like that happen to you again."

She kisses me on the cheek, "Thank you, M. So is there anything you want to know?"

I smile at her, "Just one more question. What happened with your ex, sweetheart?"

She chuckles, "I can laugh about it now, I guess. He always belittled me, talking about my weight, my looks, and my looks. I was basically his prisoner; I couldn't do anything without his permission. But after a while, things exploded; he started hitting and choking me and then cut me off from the outside world. I don't know what I did, but after almost a year of physical abuse, he got tired of me and broke up with me. He recently reached out to me and apologized, he also told me how he see where he went wrong. He fell in love with a gold digger, and she left him, so karma came around in full force. I accepted his apology, forgave him, and wished him the best. I closed that chapter, and I'm not looking back."

You can see she means every word. Kass is too forgiving; if it were up to me, he would be dead.

I kiss her cheek. "You have a big heart. Okay, I lied. I have one more question. Will you answer it for me?" The smile reaches her eyes, and she nods. Kassani Carter, will you officially be mine?"

She starts giggling and twists into my lap. "Yes, boss man. I'm yours! No take backs, baby!"

She presses her lips to mine. So this is what happiness feels like.

Kassani

(Five days later)

I feel safe and confident when I am in his lap or when his arms are around me. He shows me in many ways that he cares.

I have never had all this affection from one person; it feels right. Never in my wildest dreams would I imagine that a Bravta Don is where I would find my peace and sanity.

Over the last five days, he has come home to me after work and made me dinner every night. We talk about our days, and then we do my physical therapy. Doctor Sara was kind enough to give me an easy but effective routine to build my muscles and improve my balance. I have already seen a significant improvement; I even have more energy.

Every night, we watch a movie together and play 20 questions together. So far, I've learned that his favorite color is royal blue, which I think is cute since that's my safe color. I have also gathered that he doesn't like snap peas.

Today is a little different.

M said he has to work late, but he's having Roman come get me to the shooting range. M wants to ensure I know how to always care for myself. Roe volunteered because he knows the issues I have with my hands.

This should be fun. I feel like I'm growing stronger and becoming a better woman.

I really want to be the woman that M can count on.

He calls me his princess, but I want to be his queen.

12

Massimo

I hated that I "worked" late yesterday I wanted to see the princess shoot.

Roman texted me afterward and sent me a video.

He said she had no trouble at all, and they even bought her a pistol.

She surprises me every day.

I had to "work" late because we thought we had a lead on the sex ring we have been tracking. Turns out that it was a bad lead, and we lost five men last night.

I spent most of the night comforting the loved ones and setting them up for life so they would always be taken care of.

This is the worst part of being a Don; I can't stand when I lose men.

It breaks my heart to see families that work for me grieve and fall apart.

Normally, I would've had Roe by my side, but I'm glad he wasn't because last night, the bullet grazed me.

I would not be able to face Kass if something happened to Roe. The bullet only grazed me in the arm because Thomas stepped in; he is in the hospital recovering. Doctor Sara was able to save him. The bullet barely missed his artery.

When I got home, the princess was asleep. She had already replaced the knife with her pistol under her pillow. She was tossing just a little bit in her sleep. I have noticed that tremors have slowed since we fell into our nightly routine.

I'm not sure how today is going to go; today is Kassani's first day back at the office.

I know she's nervous about what people will think about us dating. I assured her nothing would come of it because Hailey and Keira would make sure no one said anything.

I got up early to go to my apartment and get ready. Once I was ready, I headed back to her apartment to cook her breakfast. She loves the omelets I make, so she has them for breakfast three times a week. As I'm finishing up breakfast, I see a luscious beauty walking my way in a royal blue pencil skirt and black silk shirt.

Sweetheart forgot to button a button on her top, I can see a royal blue lace bra peeking out at me. I am going to be picturing that all day.

As she saunters over to the table, I say, "Sweetheart, when did you get a new outfit? You look delicious. Did you forget a button?"

She giggles, "Thanks, boss man! I got this outfit a few days ago when I went shopping with Key. I didn't forget a button it's a fashion statement, just show a pop of color to draw people in! It certainly drew you in."

Sweetheart proceeds to unfasten another button before she starts eating her breakfast. I walk around the table and slip my arms around her torso. I whisper in her ear, "Nobody gets a peek at what's mine, princess."

I button her shirt as she replies, "Then you better show me that I belong to you, boss man."

I spin the chair around to face me. In a single swoop, I pick her up by her ass, and we switch places. She's straddling my lap. I feel her heart racing. I stroke her cheek with my index finger and slowly make my way to her lips.

I whisper, "Be careful with your words, princess. I will take what's mine."

I crash my lips to hers, entwining our tongues together, and fist her hair. Within seconds, she has my shirt open, and her hands are roaming my body; just as I start to unbutton my pants, my phone rings.

I answer it gruffly, "This better be important, Hailey." She proceeds to tell me to get my ass to the office because my meeting with the Mayor is in 30 minutes. I reply, "Yes, Mother, I'm on my way."

I hang up the phone and kiss the princess on the cheek. "Come on, sweetheart. We have to get to work. But we will continue this later."

She slowly rises from my lap, "Whatever you say, boss man." Her smile reaches her eyes.

You can tell she is more confident than a month ago.

We leave her apartment hand in hand, and it feels like nothing will stop us.

Kassani

As we make it to the office, I feel all eyes on me. M finally released my hand, but he placed his hand on my lower back as we walked into the office. He had Hailey inform HR so there would be no repercussions.

I hear the whispers.

"Why her?"

"She must be good in bed."

"He needs a whole woman not half of one!"

"She's too plump to be with Mr. Ballentine; he only dates models."

M kisses me on the forehead and heads to his meeting.

As he does, Kiera arrives at my desk and whispers in my ear, "Tune the jealousy out. M is a recluse; they are just mad that he chose you. Don't let them see you break. Don't forget we are going shopping after work since the men are working late."

Key hugs me and heads to her floor.

As she leaves, everyone's attention snaps back to me.

I wish everyone would stop staring. Anyway, I usually start my work day by completing everything. I glance at my phone, and there's a text from M.

"MS. CARTER YOU ARE NEEDED IN MY OFFICE IMMEDIATELY!" He says.

I text back, "OTW BOSSMAN!"

What could I have done to be called into the CEO's office?

Massimo

I didn't expect her to reply so fast. She probably thought she could be in trouble, but that's not true. I just wanted to spoil her.

My princess doesn't like it when I spoil her; that's due to years of trauma. But it doesn't hurt to try. If she throws it in my face, so be it; I want her to know that she is cared for.

I didn't get her much, but I was able to snag some of her favorites.

I got her a big order of California Rolls with extra soy sauce for dipping because she will share it with Kiera at lunch. I was also able to get the last of her pink and red roses, as well as her favorite chocolate. The final present I got her was a crown necklace with rubies as the crown jewels since red is her second favorite color and it's my first. I just wanted her to have something that always reminds her of me and keeps her safe.

The necklace is also for her protection. I know how rough our world can be, and I will protect her with my life. Its sensor will allow me to pull up her location at any time. Roman said it was a good idea so we could always find her if something happened.

Princess and I recently had a conversation about her safety. She said she would wear a device as long as it was fashionable, so this would suffice.

Also, hopefully, this makes up for me "working" late tonight. We have another lead, so I don't want to miss this chance to bring this ring down.

There is a soft knock on my door. I say in the gruff voice I know she craves, "Enter! Shut the door!"

As she shuts the door, I hit the hidden button on my desk to lock it. This is a special moment, and I don't want any interruptions.

She clears her throat, "You rang, boss man?"

"Yes, Ms. Carter. I called you in here to discuss your concerns." She tenses up, and I continue, "You know, the concerns you have about if I know how to listen and care for you."

As I finished speaking, I handed her the flowers and chocolate. I wink at her, "How did I do princess?"

You can see tears festering in her eyes, "Awe, M! You didn't have to do this! The flowers are beautiful, and you remembered what my favorite chocolate is! You're so sweet."

She wraps her arms around my neck, kisses my cheek, then jumps back, "Sorry, boss man! I forgot we are at work! I will contain my joy."

I chuckle and fix a strand of her hair, "Oh princess, you lost it over a few flowers and a box of treats I can't wait to see how you react to your final present."

She gets giddy, "M, you are spoiling me! I kind of like it! Let me see, baby!"

I respond, "Cover your eyes."

She places her hands over her eyes and says, "I am ready, baby!"

That sounds so hot and sexy.

I spin her around so her back is touching my chest. She wiggles her plump ass against my crotch and snickers.

I slip the necklace from the box, gently clasp it around her neck, and lock it in place with the key.

I whisper in her ear, "This is the safety necklace we talked about getting. It can only be removed if it is unlocked, so if someone tries to take it off of you, they will not be able to without the key. Also, the chain is indestructible. But princess, it is not as beautiful as you. Open your eyes."

I placed her in front of my free-standing mirror.

Her breath hitches. "Oh, M! It's gorgeous, and your favorite color is also my second favorite! How sweet and thoughtful!"

She leans against me, just taking in the moment, and then turns around quickly, softly placing her arms around my neck and saying, "I love you, boss man."

As I lean in to kiss her, I grunt, "I love you more, princess."

13

Kassani

Boss man is kissing me like there is no tomorrow!

He loves me; he actually loves me!

His hand is roaming all over my body.

He flicks open my shirt and whispers, "I have been picturing this sexy body of yours all morning! Does the bra match the panties?"

"Why don't you find out, boss man?" I sigh.

I rub my ass all over his crotch and move his hands to the edge of my skirt.

He doesn't hesitate; his hand finds the zipper at the back of my skirt and throws it to the floor. My panties match my bra, but they are royal blue lace cheeksters. M has my ass in his hands.

He grunts, "I will never look at royal blue the same again! Princess, your body is perfection."

He is clawing my back from my neck to my ass.

It gives me the shivers. It's like he knows where and when to touch me. He's being very gentle but assertive.

He spins me around and says, "This is your only chance to back out, princess. What do you say?"

He's asking me if I want him to stop. Has he lost it?

Before I answer him, I start unbuttoning his shirt, then glide my hand to his crotch and unfasten his belt and pants.

I hear myself say, "Take me, boss man! I'm yours!"

He pounces on me, and before I know it I'm sitting bare-assed on his desk.

He swiftly removed my bra and panties, and he now is pulling his underwear to his ankles.

He positions himself even with my entrance and grunts, "Last chance, princess; once I fully make you mine, no one can have you."

I loudly sigh, "Boss man, if you don't take me now, you can't have me!"

He grunts and pulls me forward, at first he's teasing my entry with his penis then he can't hold back any longer.

He grabs my ass with both hands and thrusts me forward.

It's like he was made for me!

He thrusts faster and harder while kissing my neck and caressing my breasts.

I'm pretty sure everyone in the office can hear us, with him grunting and me moaning at the top of my lungs.

But I don't care; this feels right!

It's so hot and dirty! I never thought I would be in this situation, but he makes regrets impossible!

His lips move from my cheek to my breast; he begins to suck.

Damn! That makes me even wetter; his lips are magic.

Is this what sex is supposed to feel like?

I have been with only one person, but it has never felt like this!

Was I the problem?

Get out of your head, Kass!

Don't make M do all the work!

I'm so close that I can feel it, but I need to take care of M. I push him off me and glands in his chair. I glide off of the desk and sink onto my knees and give him a wicked grin, I wrap my hand around the head of his penis and guide it to my mouth.

I hear M gasping as my tongue wraps around the head. His grunts turn into loud moans.

His hands gripped my hair and held me in place. This feels so dirty but it's turning me on more.

I lick from base to tip, and as I pump his dick with my hand, he is squirming in his seat. I can feel that he's on the verge of cumming.

I quickly release his dick and plop onto his lap and guide him into my entrance.

Straddling him is such a turn-on!

His big biceps wrap around me, and he places his face in my chest to muffle his cries.

I am riding his dick like there is no end in sight, except I feel my orgasm building. I keep riding him faster and harder, and I slam my lips against him to muffle my moan.

Just as I think my orgasm is ending M grabs my ass and thrusts even harder bringing it right back and we crash over the edge together.

I'm in a sweaty, blissful state when the office phone rings.

M answers swiftly and professionally.

"Yes, how can I assist you? Fine! Next time, call my cell. I'll be ready in twenty minutes. Yes, mother." He smirks. "That was Hailey. I have a meeting in thirty minutes. She likes to bug me. I am sorry, my love. I wish I had more time. This is not what I had planned for our first time. But do you want to know a secret?"

I press my body against his and reply, "Today was perfect my love. What is it, baby?"

He grabs my ass, "Go right through that door, and you can use my shower; it's fully stocked. Also, I forgot to tell you that my office is a soundproof princess so no need to be embarrassed. I will get dressed and head to my meeting across town; when you are showered, I left your lunch under my desk. I happened to get enough for Kiera, too."

He kisses me one last time as I walk to the shower, so this is how it feels to be loved.

I feel like royalty.

14

Massimo

What a morning! My princess gave herself to me.

She is mine, which means no one can have her, and I'll protect her with all I have.

I was very shocked that we ended up having intercourse in my office, I am not complaining. But I didn't consider that my sweetheart would be that adventurous, considering she was only with the abusive man.

She took my breath away.

She was very responsive and attentive to my needs. I hated to leave her after that, but I had to get across town to meet up with Dorian and Marco.

We are still following that trafficking ring. We were able to put a woman on the inside. She volunteered against my better judgment, but she is a killing machine. Rachel has been a part of the Bratva world since birth. Her father trained beside my father, and Asia will not fail. Asia is our number one spy and has done several missions for us.

She is also secretly in love with Roman.

This is why Roman is not on this mission. I know he has feelings for Asia but will not admit them. So, if he sees her like this, he may go ballistic. Asia sent us the coded message earlier today.

Jared is taking me there to meet Dorian and Marco.

I have a feeling tonight is going to be messy. But I convinced Kiera to stay with Kassani so she wouldn't be alone tonight. Marco hides nothing from Kiera, and she's a badass in her own right.

We arrive at the meet-up point, and we are all armed, we only brought fifteen men with us for this mission.

We each are packing a knife, gun, and blow torch. He have to stay focused and get these women out.

Asia contacted us with urgent news: tonight, they plan to transport twenty women to an undisclosed location.

She also shared the address of a house where several others are being kept against their will.

In response, we quickly mobilized a larger team to raid the house. After a tense operation, we managed to rescue all fifty women held inside. They are now en route to our Hope Shelter, where we have made extensive preparations for their arrival.

Our facility is stocked with cozy beds, warm meals, and fresh clothing, ensuring they feel safe and cared for as they begin to heal from their ordeal.

Marco leads one team and Dorian and I lead the other two teams, Asia just texted again it's show time. Asia said there are three guards, one at the entrance, and three on the inside. This should be an in-and-out mission.

As we enter we easily take out the three outside guards. We move to the interior of the building we see the other guards charging at us, I'm a superior marksman. Three shots is all it takes, dead on impact. I only shoot to kill when I have to.

After all the guards are dead, we gather all the women and head to the Hope shelter. I sent the coded text to our clean-up crew; they will take care of this in less than an hour.

Doctor Sara and her team met us at the shelter to assess all the women. She never lets us down, either.

Five women had to be taken to the hospital. Three of them were dehydrated and malnourished, so Sara wanted to get fluids and vitamins in them and keep them for observation. The other two had serious scars and burns all over their bodies, if I hadn't killed those men they would be dead. Any man who lays a malicious finger on a woman deserves death.

Once we settle all the women and gather all their information, we head to Dorian's place to regroup and debrief.

It's our tradition; these men are my family.

We eat, smoke cigars, and drink whiskey until none of us can stay awake.

Tomorrow is another day for us to make a difference, and we will eliminate one threat at a time.

15

Kassani

What an afternoon and night!

Kiera forced me to shop until I couldn't shop anymore.

I got a few office outfits and a few more formal dresses just in case I needed them. I was even able to sneak in some new lingerie. I didn't want Key to see it because I would be so embarrassed.

Key also opened my eyes to how much money I am making at Ballentine Industries.

I make fifty-five dollars an hour! I'm in complete shock! I have been budgeting my spending, thinking I only make twenty dollars an hour, because I was afraid I wouldn't be able to pay rent. No matter what, M will not be allowed to pay my bills. I have taken care of myself all these years, so that won't stop now.

It's been instilled in me to make my own money, that way I don't have to rely on anyone else for my needs or wants. Due to my condition, I feel like I have been a burden on my family because they have taken care of me, with all of the extra expenses since I was 18 months old. It's my responsibility to give that back to them and help them whenever possible. It's taken a lot for me to accept the gifts M got me, but I will repay him.

When I was out with Key, I found a gift I think he will love: cuff links that match the necklace he gave me! I'm going to give them to him today at lunch. I also got him a red and black tie with a crown on it. I want him to realize how committed I am to him.

When we got back from shopping, we hung out the rest of the night at my place. We talked about each other's relationships, and then we drank the night away! We both fell asleep on the couch. It was like we were teenagers again at a sleepover at my Nana's. Those were the simple days when we had no responsibilities.

After getting ready for the day, we hear our phones go off. Before I look at mine, I see Key's mood shrink. She looks a little sad, and I wonder what happened.

I glance at my phone, and there's a text from M.

"PRINCESS CANNOT MEET FOR LUNCH! EMER-GENCY! HOPEFULLY, I WILL SEE YOU TOMORROW."

Wow. It must be on the Bratva front because he never misses a chance to spend time together. But I have to be prepared for this, this is the life when you are dating a Don.

I look at Key, "What did your message say, Key?"

She sighs, "How much does Massimo tell you about the Bratva?"

I shrug, "Not much why, what is going on?"

She urges me to sit down, "Last night, they saved a bunch of women that were part of a sex trafficking ring they have been tracking for some time now. Some of the women started showing signs this morning of poisoning, and they were rushed to the hospital. Marco and Massimo are returning to where the women were kept to see what they can find."

What in the hell!

Why wouldn't M tell me that's what going on?

"How many women were involved?"

She looks at the floor. "Seventy total. They got them all out. But this morning, at least twenty of them were showing signs of poisoning, except for the agent that they had on the inside. So, the three of them are trying to figure out what happened while Doctor Sara tries to flush the poison out of all these women. They were expecting to be home today. Sorry, Kass, but we can go to the gym and spend the day together again if you want."

When she sees my panic setting in, she taps my shoulder, "Breathe. They will save them. Let's get you to physical therapy, and we will go from there. Trust Marco and Massimo; they have been through a lot worse."

I nod, "Okay let's go. But I definitely need to go to boxing class today. I need to hit something."

Boxing has become a stress reliever for me, and M thinks it's sexy.

Key laughs, "Okay, let's go, girl!"

Two girls are off to fight out our frustrations until our men return.

They will return.

I must stay positive.

My King will return to me.

Massimo

After yesterday, if there is ever another sex trafficking ring in my city, there will be hell to pay!

Doctor Sara was able to save all but five women. Those five women were drinking too much of the contaminated alcohol.

Whoever was behind this ring poisoned the alcohol. Asia is a picky drinker, so she never drank any of it. She said if it's not vodka, she doesn't want it. After word spread around our family, Roman blew up my phone.

Roman has been checking in on Asia every ten minutes. Why doesn't he just call her? He needs to get his head out of his ass!

I told Asia to call him and she laughed at me, I swear they are made for each other.

My phone goes off; I ignore it. But Marco comes running in my direction.

"Boss code red!"

What the hell?

Code red means kidnapping of one of us.

"What? Who? What do we got?" I am tense as I look around and ensure everyone is accounted for.

Marco forces me to sit down.

"Brother, it's Kassani. Kiera said she was supposed to meet her at the gym again since we didn't come home last night. But she never showed. She had Jared let her into her apartment. There was evidence of a struggle. They found a syringe on the floor that contained a strong sedative."

My breathing goes ragged, "You are lying! There's no way someone kidnapped my princess!"

He pats my shoulder, "We checked the apartment security system and cameras, too. Massimo, it's true. A figure in a black hoodie with a white mask covering their face. The mask had a red cross on the forehead."

Why does a red cross sound familiar?

I jump up from my seat. "I'm calling Roman now. Let's head to her apartment and see what we can find. We have to find her!"

I call Roman, and he says he will be there in five minutes.

He's just as pissed as I am.

Whoever took her is in for a rude awakening!

Not only will they suffer at my hands, but Kassani has been training her ass off. She said she no longer wants anyone to have to take care of her fully.

No matter what she says I will always take care of her.

When we arrived at Kassani's apartment, someone called the police. Two police officers are talking to Sarah in the lobby. Before we even make it upstairs, Roman is with us. Sarah nodded in my direction, letting me know she would keep the police downstairs until we gave her the signal. If she can't keep them there, she will call me.

We finally get to her apartment. The first thing I see is that her door is intact, so either they had a key, or Kassani let them in. As we walk in, we see that they were not trying to take anything; everything that is broken is clearly from a struggle. At least my princess didn't go easily.

On the floor there is a knife with blood on it, Roman grabs it and bags it. He will take it straight to our private lab.

He sighs, "This better not be her blood, if it is I call dibs on the asshole that stabbed her."

I say to him, "I'm pretty sure that's not her blood. That's her favorite kitchen knife, she probably stabbed the attacker. She's been taking defense classes and training with knives and boxing. Whoever took her better watch their face."

There are only signs of a struggle in the living room. Her room door is shut but I open it just to make sure. I enter her bedroom everything looks normal except there's a red gift bag and card on her bed. The card has a big red M on it.

I pick it up and open it. It's a red card with an M on the outside and on the inside there is her beautiful calligraphy.

"My King,

I know little gifts will be nothing compared to everything you already have, but I wanted to get you something to show you how much I care. They are your favorite colors, and I put just a little thought and love into them. You rule the Bratva and my heart. Never forget that my love for you stems from your kind and loving heart, as well as your powerful mind and body. I will love you forever and always.

Love,

Your Princess"

She really has broken through my cold, black heart. Tears slide down my face as I open the gift bag. Inside, I find a stunning red tie with a crown on it and cuff links that match her necklace perfectly.

Her necklace!

I pull out my phone and open my Safety First application.

16

Kassani

As I slowly come to, the last thing I remember is stabbing my ex in the shoulder.

I stupidly opened the door, thinking it was Key at the door because I was late for the gym.

But it was an asshole, one who recently apologized, at my door wearing a white mask with a red cross on the forehead. He pushed his way in and only then did he remove the mask. He had the audacity to ask me if I missed him.

My fight or flight reflexes kicked in, and I grabbed my kitchen knife and stabbed him in the shoulder.

That sent him over the edge; he threw me through my glass coffee table. I can still feel a piece of glass in my shoulder; if I survive this, I will kill Jacob. Never again will I forgive so easily.

I noticed my surroundings almost immediately; this was a new place to me.

It's damp and dark, with only a small window, possibly twelve feet in the air. There was no way, if my hands and feet weren't tied, I would be able to reach that window.

All I smell in here is moist air and decaying rats.

My hands are chained to the wall, and my feet are bound with rope, Jacob must've told him how I thought which is why they restrained me so much, which was a good move on their part because whoever did this is going to.

As I gather my thoughts, a pounding knock sounds on the door, and Jacob enters.

"Wakey wakey, sleepyhead! Aren't you glad to see my smiling face? When we're done with you, you won't be recognizable." He laughs.

" I would say it's nice to see you again, but that would be a lie. I forgave you for what you did before, but this is unforgivable. You better hope that you kill me. I manage to get out of here, or even just get my hands or legs free you will die. After everything you put me through, I have done nothing to you. You deserve anything that comes your way."

I stare him straight in the eye.

I refuse to back down.

I am not that weak woman he could once control.

He chuckles, "Darling, you couldn't hurt a fly! You stabbing me earlier was pure luck. But let me tell you, I don't want to see you suffer, but my fiancée wants to see your man suffer. And I will do anything to make her happy."

"Your fiancée, huh? Well, she must be a psychopath to have you kidnap somebody's girlfriend just for revenge. Do you think that this was a good idea? Do you think that you will survive this today? Do you understand whose girlfriend you kidnapped?"

As soon as I finish speaking, a voice sounds in the doorway, "Little girl, I know exactly who I'm dealing with. But you're completely right; I am a psychopath. I have no heart, and I show no mercy. Everything I do is to satisfy revenge. The revenge I'm looking for is on your dear sweet Massimo. He's gone soft, especially if you think that cold-hearted monster fell in love with someone like you. You are nothing but a pathetic little burden. The only reason you were able to injure Jacob is because he's not a part of this world and he thinks with his heart, but I don't. My heart's been cold since the day Massimo left me."

I chuckled, " OK now that makes sense! I know exactly who you are. My best friend told me everything she knows about you. You are Rosalie Angelo; you thought you could steal the Bratva from under Massimo. And the only reason he didn't kill you was because he doesn't hurt women. But you better hope I don't get free. You can do whatever you like to me, but now, no mercy will come your way. I may look like a burden to you, but that's because you're like everybody else. See how strong I can be. But Massimo does, and that's why he loves me."

She cackled, "There's no way he loves a handicap, frail, insolent woman! He needs a woman who can stand by his side through everything; you can barely stand up enough to walk, let alone stand by his side and help him through the dangers of this world."

"You mean, he needs a woman, you? Yes, you are a woman who can fight and stand on her own. But you're also a woman who sleeps with whoever she can. Oh yeah, my best friend was kind enough to tell me your history and how much you cheated on Massimo. I have way more dignity than you do. We are completely different people. Cheating is not in my vocabulary. You and Jacob, y'all belong together; y'all both like to cheat just as much. Thank you for taking that boy off my hands. But whatever you are planning, I'm sure M will be ten steps ahead of you."

She doesn't scare me, she just a vengeful woman with nothing better to do.

She stormed her overly done-up body over to me.

She kneeled and smacked me across the face, and whispered, "No matter what, Massimo will be mine again. I will not let a disabled brat stand in my way. You were not made for this world but I was, so back off or I will kill you."

Before she even has a chance to get up I head butt her and sweep her feet from underneath her.

"Don't underestimate me, Rose. I'm capable of more than you know. M is mine, and I will not back down."

She stumbles backward and yells at Jacob, "She gets no food until I say so!"

All the while blood is pouring from her nose, I'm sure that I broke it. That will leave a mark.

When she stumbled, I was able to snatch her pointy cross necklace off with my teeth. I flung it behind me so they wouldn't notice. It is sharp enough for me to be able to saw my feet apart. As soon as I can do that, I'll be able to free my hands as well.

I have a plan. Rosalie posted a kid outside the door of my cell, I am very fluent in pressure points. One touch and it's nighty night for him.

I was able to get free! I grabbed the kid's key before he passed out, and I grabbed his gun as well. I am an excellent shot; let's hope I don't have to use it.

I don't know where or what to do, but I will try to escape.

I'll follow the voices and try to stay out of sight.

My hand touches my necklace.

I know my king will be here soon.

17

Massimo

Rosalie better hope and pray my princess is unharmed.

If she touched a heart on her head, I will end Rosalie.

Why in the hell would she kidnap Kassani?

Kass is innocent, but that's always what Rosalie got off on preying on the innocent.

This has to be about revenge.

I had Marco do some digging, and he found that we had missed a big piece of the puzzle. Turns out that Rosalie killed her father a month ago.

She had found out he was so fed up with her games that he was no longer leaving the Bratva to her. Unless she got married to one of his men, of course, she was against it even though she was sleeping with most of his men already.

That's why she reappeared. Her father didn't leave a will, so it automatically became hers. Now she's seeking me out because she wants full control over my city. That will never happen. I have plans to make Kassani my Bratva Queen. Rosalie used me for what she could gain. Kassani is with me to make me a better man.

Rosalie made me into an uninteresting asshole. A part of me feels that she is not capable of love. But this time I'm prepared for anything she tries to throw at me.

I have Hailey and Asia as my backup as well as Dorian, Roman, and Marco. Rosalie knows nothing of Hailey and Asia's abilities; she better be scared. It's Hailey for whom she needs to watch out.

Hailey has always hated Rosalie. Hailey caught Rosalie cheating on me, and I didn't believe her.

Our plan involves walking into the compound.

The girls are scoping out the compound and giving us all the information. I know Rosalie expects me to come charging to rescue my princess, but she won't expect Massimo the Monster.

Massimo the Monster is an asshole to the fullest, he gives no fucks and he knows what to do to put everyone in line.

I was the Monster for two years after Rosalie broke me.

Now, she will get to see that side of me. I am going to make her wish she never betrayed me. I remember all her kinks and all the little triggers that give away her lies.

Get ready, Rosalie, you're about to bow to the King.

Kassani

As I walk the halls of this unfamiliar place, I hear strange noises throughout. As I walk past one door, I hear moaning and skin slapping together. The next door, all I hear is metal clanging together and screaming, it sounds like someone is about to die.

Is this what a Bratva is really like? Who's the Don? Would they really let all kinds of exploits go on like this?

I'm looking for a place to hide until I can find a safe exit. I found a big empty closet, which is actually in a big open ballroom. It's a massive room, but what was suspicious was that there was only one thing in there—a very extravagant throne.

You know what it doesn't matter as long as no one finds me in here. My legs are shaky, there's plenty of space in here so I'm going to sit down and rest my legs while I hide. I have to make my way back to Massimo.

I can't let this be how we end.

I want a life with him, and even if it means getting down and dirty, I'm willing to take that risk. No matter what, I will stand by his side, legal or illegal. I'll be the one he can count on.

As I get seated I hear a few familiar voices. It sounds like it's Rosalie and a group of men. It is!!! I can identify Rosalie and Massimo but the other people present haven't said anything yet.

What is M doing and why does Rosalie sound like she's trying to seduce him?

I'm not going to panic! I am going to sit here until the time is right. I can watch everything unfold right here from the crack of the door.

Rosalie better watch what she says, I am at the perfect angle where I won't miss.

Massimo

Rosalie is still as self-absorbed as ever. I checked the application before we walked in, and my princess was watching our every move. How would Rosalie not be aware that her prisoner was moving about her compound?

I see Kass watching. Rosalie has her back turned, so I quickly do the symbol that she and Kiera use to let her know that I see her. This should be fun; I'm about to put Rosalie through it.

"Massimo baby, I'm glad you came to see me. You're looking as sexy as ever. What brings you by, handsome?" She says as she sits on her flashy throne.

I huff, "I heard you took something that belongs to my crew. What made you think I wouldn't come? We want her back, now!"

She laughed, "But baby, we could have some fun with her. Wouldn't you like her to watch us play together? I'll let you be in control this time."

Before I can answer, Roman replies, "Not on my watch, but that's my sister. Just give her to me, and I'll leave so y'all can work out y'all sexual tension. I want no part of that."

"Awe, poor Roe Roe, he's a prude." Rosalie snickers.

"Shut up, Rosalie. If it weren't my sister you took, I wouldn't even be looking at your ugly face. By the way, what happened to your nose? Did you run into the door?" Roe asks.

Rosalie scoffed quietly, "Your bitch of a sister head-butted me."

I step towards her, "You want to repeat that? Are you insulting someone in my crew? What did you do to deserve it? Be your bitchy self? If you harmed her, I will let Roman loose."

She chuckles, "Roman? What about you, Massimo? I'll let you ravage me."

I maintain my composure when really I'm ready to throw up and kill her.

"Baby, I want to do more than ravage you. Mangle is more suitable for you, my dear. You have been a pain in my ass for far too long. I should have killed when your father permitted me to."

She flinches, "He what? My father would never allow that! You're a lying asshole!"

I smirk, "If I recall correctly, he said, "That traitor is no daughter of mine; do what you want with her."

She snatches her knife from her boot and presses it against my throat, "I dare you to try. If that's what you came here to do, fine, but all I have is scream one word, and you all will be dead."

"Do I look scared? Do you really think you scare us? Do you think we came unprepared? You, my dear, forget. This is my city. Have you found the mole that I planted in your Bratva?"

She looks flabbergasted, "Mole? Massimo, there's no way you infiltrated my ranks. Who is it? No, you are lying! You're not smarter than me!"

She goes to grab her gun, and as she raises it to shoot me, we hear a silent gunshot.

Before I can grasp the situation, Rosalie falls backward onto the ballroom floor.

As she hits the floor blood pools around her head, that was a kill shot. I scramble to see where it came from.

Right in front of me is the culprit.

She is not concerned; she looks content.

Her eyes locked mine as she says, "Nobody threatens my King."

Where did this side of my princess come from?

I'm a little scared, but turned on.

There she is, the QUEEN has arrived.

18

Kassani

With disbelief and wonder, I never imagined that this day would eventually arrive.

At this moment, I come alive with a newfound strength and unwavering self-confidence.

My heart swells with pride as I realize that I have accomplished the impossible and saved my King from harm's way.

The heavy weight of being handicapped has been lifted, and now a new sense of confidence emerges - the confidence of being capable, competent, and empowered, regardless of any physical or mental disabilities.

With this renewed sense of self, this individual with disabilities can confidently take on any challenge and overcome any obstacle that comes my way.

I acted promptly to prevent a woman from taking the life of my beloved King. She had a weapon in hand, poised to strike, but I couldn't let her succeed in her deadly mission. I stood up to defend my King, and although it was a difficult decision, I had to take her down to ensure his safety. I would never tolerate anyone trying to harm him, and I was prepared to do whatever it takes to protect him.

I feel anxious and uncertain about how Massimo will react after what I've done for him. Despite making this significant sacrifice, I fear he may not love me like he did before. The reason for my apprehension is that I'm not sure how acceptable it is in Massimo's world for women to kill.

I hope he understands my intentions and doesn't misunderstand my actions. Despite the fact that I have only a few drops of blood on me, my appearance is quite disheveled, to say the least.

The experience has left me feeling traumatized, and I am struggling to come to terms with what has happened to me. I am trying my best to remain calm and composed, but it is proving incredibly difficult, given the circumstances. As I loosen my grip on the gun, it slips from my fingers and lands with a dull thud on the ground.

I hastily nudge it towards Massimo with the tip of my shoe, hoping to relinquish the weapon's weight as quickly as possible.

But as the adrenaline fades, I feel my confidence ebb away, leaving me vulnerable and exposed. A sense of impending doom washes over me, and I feel myself being pulled into the abyss of my own mind - a dark and treacherous place where I am lost and alone. I stood there, feeling small and vulnerable, with my eyes cast downward and my arms wrapped tightly around my body.

It was as if I was a prisoner to my own thoughts, unable to escape the fear that had taken hold of me.

I couldn't shake the feeling that something was wrong, that Massimo's love for me was slipping away.

It was a thought that had been gnawing at me for days, and now it seemed to be consuming me completely. I felt helpless and alone, uncertain of what the future held.

As I delve into the depths of my mind, exploring the twists and turns of my thoughts, I suddenly feel a warm embrace from behind.

A pair of strong arms wrap around me, gently pulling me back to the surface of reality.

The touch is reassuring, grounding me in the present moment and reminding me of the comfort of human connection.

As I lift my gaze to the heavens above, my eyes rest upon the majestic figure of the Bratva King, towering above me like a towering colossus.

He is the undisputed ruler of my heart, a symbol of strength, power, and unwavering loyalty. His presence commands respect, and I am grateful to be in his presence, basking in the warm glow of his glory.

He holds me tenderly, his warm embrace making me feel safe and loved. As he lifts me up, I hear the soft rustling of his shirt and feel the strength in his arms.

With a gentle and reassuring voice, he whispers in my ear, "Let's take you home, my Queen," and I know that I am exactly where I belong.

19

Massimo

Kassani shot Rosalie.

The clean-up crew has taken care of everything.

The compound and the people are all gone, thanks to Jared.

As we make our way towards the apartment complex, I cannot help but notice the sorrowful expression on my queen's face.

Her eyes are downcast, and her once radiant demeanor seems to have faded away.

I understand it is my duty to bring back her light and re-assure her that everything will be alright.

I must find the right words to say and be the support she needs in this moment of distress.

"My love, you are troubled. I am here to listen and support you. Would you like to share what is on your mind? I care about your well-being and want to help however I can."

As I spoke kind words to her, she shifted in her seat and looked at me with a questioning expression.

"Do you love me any less?" she asked.

I reassured her with a smile and tried to continue speaking.

Suddenly, she interrupted me with a serious question, "Are women allowed to participate in the Bratva world?"

Her eyes were filled with curiosity and a hint of concern, awaiting my response. "Kass, I understand your concern, but I assure you there is no need to worry. Hailey, who may not appear very intimidating, is a lethal weapon. She was with us during the rescue mission to save you and was crucial to its success. I want to highlight that our team comprises many highly skilled and capable women who work with us and contribute significantly to our cause. Your skills today showed me how much I need you by my side."

Recognition flickers, "Massimo, you need a handicapped woman by your side and not a model?"

I gently caressed her cheek and whispered, "Your beauty is unparalleled. No one compares to you."

As we approached her apartment building, I turned to her and asked, "Would you be willing to come over to my place instead?"

Her face lights up with a smile, and she nods eagerly.

We continue walking hand in hand, taking in the sights and sounds of the bustling city around us.

As we approach the entrance, I can feel my heart beating faster with anticipation.

We step inside and make our way to the hidden elevator, ready to embark on the next chapter of our adventure together. Compared to others, we haven't been together long, but I want to make her my queen and my wife.

I'm nervous, but my feelings are genuine.

After buying her a beautiful necklace, I decided to have a one-of-a-kind engagement ring custom-made.

I've been waiting for the right moment to ask her, and I believe that moment has finally arrived.

Kassani

It is strange that we always stay at my apartment, and he doesn't want to stay now.

I wonder if something is bothering Massimo that he is not telling me. Maybe he is tired of staying at my place and misses his home. However, I am not too worried because everything feels comfortable as long as he is by my side.

Today has been an eventful day for me.

Despite my handicap, I realized that there are still many things that I can do and accomplish.

Massimo has also assured me that I have a place in Bratva if I ever need it. I never expected that I would have to take someone's life, but I have been training to defend myself in case of such situations.

Do I feel regret for what I did?
No. Threatening someone I love is like violating the golden rule, and I would retake the same action to protect them.

I wasn't meant to be a part of this life, but now I find myself standing by Massimo's side.

Whether he needs my help or wants me to be there for him, I'm ready and willing to support him.

I've realized that I can do anything I set my mind to.

For the first time in my life, I feel like I am being treated as an equal by someone I am with. He respects me and doesn't make me feel self-conscious.

He never tries to control what I eat or wear. I feel free from the prison I used to be in, and it's an amazing feeling.

Despite everything that has happened, I still believe that the good in Massimo's Bratva outweighs the bad.

It's not easy dealing with violence and illegal activities, but I know I can handle it. I never thought I would fall in love with someone whom people call the Monster, especially given my history with horrible men. But I don't regret loving Massimo.

We finally reached his apartment, and as we stepped inside, the sweet aroma of rose petals and candles filled the air.

He turned to me, his eyes gleaming with affection, and spoke softly, "My love, you must be exhausted. Why don't you take a relaxing shower, and I will prepare a romantic dinner for us?" He reached into a shopping bag and pulled out a few elegant outfits, "I bought you these, pick one to wear after your shower, and we'll have a lovely night together."

I couldn't resist but give him a gentle kiss on the lips before making my way to the shower, feeling grateful for his thoughtfulness and love.

20

Massimo

The shower turns on, prompting me to hurry and get everything ready.

Kass is easy to please and very lovable.

Her favorite dinner is spaghetti and meatballs, which I make by hand.

I prepare the sauce just as my mother taught me.

While the noodles are cooking and the sauce is simmering, I change into my suit and put on the tie and cuff links my sweetheart gave me.

As I gaze at the custom crown ring, I pray she will say yes. Though I'm not religious, life without Kass feels dull and gloomy.

She brings so much joy and energy into my life that I can't imagine living without her. I have never laughed as much as I do with her.

Unfortunately, I couldn't ask her father for permission to marry her.

However, I did ask Roman, and he was very supportive. He even offered to take care of her dad. But he warned me that Kass's dad is very strict and that no man she has ever brought home has been able to win him over.

After my timer buzzes, I am relieved that dinner is finally ready.

I carefully plate everything on the table, arranging it like a chef in a five-star restaurant.

Despite being a skilled and emotionless criminal interrogator, I feel nervous and jittery in front of the woman I love.

As I wait for her to arrive, I pat the ring in my pocket, feeling reassured by its presence.

Finally, my queen enters the living area, looking stunning in a new outfit.

She admires my outfit and compliments me, saying my fashion sense is better than hers.

She decided to try a different color tonight and loves how it looks on her.

She is wearing the red jumpsuit I selected, which fits her perfectly.

I purchased two identical jumpsuits for her - one in royal blue and the other in scarlet red. I initially thought she would prefer the royal blue one, but to my surprise, she chose my favorite color - red.

"I overheard you asking Kiera at work the other day if she thought you would look good in designer clothes. I wanted to let you know that you look very elegant and stylish. You picked my favorite color for your outfit."

I picked up my tie and showed her how it matched her jumpsuit.

"Oh, M! I was excited to give you those gifts. Do you like them?" She puts her hand on my chest and looks up at me.

"I love them; you make me feel like royalty."

I tuck a stray hair behind her ear; she always shivers when I do. "Let's eat before it gets cold."

As I pull out her chair, she turns into a giddy child; her favorite meal is devoured in less than eight minutes.

Kassani

He knows the way to my heart: food.

You can taste the hand-battered love in every bite.

He treats me like royalty; he's the only king I need.

Life has a weird way of telling you what you need.

When Roe and I went shooting, he told me not to break Massimo's heart because, this time, M was genuinely happy. He said that he hopes that M will be part of our family one day. I found that strange.

It was like Roe knew something that he wasn't telling me. I gazed lovingly at M and said, "Thank you for dinner, my love. Today has been a nightmare, but you make everything better."

I place my hand over him, and he replies, "Don't think I forgot, sweetheart. Your chocolate cake is in the fridge. Why don't you go get used to it some?"

When he mentioned chocolate cake, my mouth started watering uncontrollably.

He knows me too well - I have a major sweet tooth and can never resist a delicious chocolatey treat or a scrumptious cake.

Without wasting any more time, I quickly get up from my seat and rush towards the fridge.

As I open the door, I feel the cool air hit my face, and I can't help but feel excited. My eyes scan the shelves, looking for anything that resembles my favorite dessert.

Finally, I spot a beautifully decorated chocolate cake sitting in the corner.

I can hardly contain my excitement as I grab a fork and dig in.

As I turned around quickly, my mouth full of cake, I asked, "Did I ever tell you that I love you?"

M is out of my sight. Where did he go?

I move forward slowly.

Oh my goodness!

There's M!

This can't be happening!

My handsome Zeus is on one knee.

"Kassani Renee Carter, I know our relationship may not be the most traditional one, but having you in my life has made it better in countless ways. I promise to always treat you like royalty and to cook for you whenever you desire. Will you do me the honor of becoming my wife?"

As he opens the box, I instinctively place my hand on my necklace. I feel complete.

The ring he chose matches my necklace perfectly.

I carefully placed the cake on the kitchen counter, I say, "But only on one condition."

He appears shocked and sad. "What's your condition, my Queen?"

I sit on his knee and kiss him passionately. "Don't make me wait. Legally make me your Queen tomorrow."

He eagerly grabs me and pulls me close, his eyes sparkling with excitement.

With a wide grin on his face, he says, "I can't wait any longer. Let's go to the courthouse tomorrow morning right after it opens. That way, we can make it official and start our forever together."

He plants a series of kisses on my face as I giggle and try to catch my breath.

The anticipation of our future fills me with joy, and I can't help but smile back at him. I feel grateful to have found someone who loves me so deeply and passionately.

My life will be sweet and royal.

21

Epilogue- Kassani

As we walk into the courthouse, a small group follows close behind.

Marco and Kiera, Roman, Hailey, Jared, and Dorian protect us and see us off to forever as husband and wife.

We all file into Judge Dean's chambers.

Massimo loves me so much that he even agreed to my sneaky but loving plan.

I made sure Kiera wore white, too.

It's always been our dream to get married together.

Kiera hasn't noticed that Massimo and Marco are wearing matching suits.

We called the judge earlier and, with Marco's help, took care of all the paperwork so Kay and Key can live their childhood dreams today.

As Judge Dean begins, Kiera goes to move over by everyone else, but Marco holds her in place.

"Dearly beloved, we are gathered here today to witness the union of Kassani and Massimo, as well as Kiera and Marco."

As I turn my head to look at Key, I notice tears streaming down her face.

Her eyes are red and puffy, and her cheeks are wet with tears.

I can tell she's crying more now than when we first arrived.

Our eyes meet, and I can see her expression of pain, sadness, and joy.

Despite the noise and chaos around us, we feel like the only two people in the room. I reach out to her, offering a comforting hand on her shoulder.

She mouths as Marco holds her up, "I love you always."

I blow her a kiss and pay attention to the judge.

Now, we will always share a birthday and an anniversary.

"I now pronounce you both husband and wife! You may kiss your brides!"

Massimo dips me like the Queen he's made me into and kisses me like he will never let me go.

You can tell Marco and Massimo and thick as thieves, Marco dipped Key with the same amount of love and adoration.

Society's standards define my disability, but my love has redefined my life and strength.

I now reign over my life and a small part of the Bratva.

My reign is reimagined, forever and always.

With love and support, we can achieve our happy ending.

About the Author

*SUMMER N DAWN IS A SMALL-TOWN AU-THOR LIVING OUT HER DREAM!
SHE LOVES TO CREATE WORLDS THAT PEOPLE CAN RELATE TO AND FIT INTO.
SHE HAS CEREBRAL PALSY, AND SHE DOESN'T LET THAT STOP HER.
HER DISABILITY IS NEVER A CRUTCH BUT A CROWN SHE WEARS WITH PRIDE.*